In the Kitchen With Linda

Advance Praise

for *In the Kitchen With Linda: Loving Memories, Favorite Recipes, and Handy Hints*

"Oh, what fun I had through many tears as memories joyful and tender flowed through my heart. I'm so honored to be part of Linda's cooking journey."

—**Marion Klein Bieksha,** *friend*

"Over the past thirty or so years, Linda and Jerry Carsman have hosted us for many of the terrific meals spelled out in her recent book... which has left us drooling. Her skills in the kitchen are more than worthy of this new cookbook, putting on paper dishes for all to emulate. Enjoy!"

—**Steve and Sherry Raffin,** *friends*

"Most people think their mom is the best cook ever, and I'm no different. My sisters, friends, and I always raved about her cooking. I wanted to preserve her amazing recipes and tips, so *In the Kitchen with Linda* was born. This true labor of love is a delightful mix of stories, life lessons, and mouth-watering dishes from my mom to you. *B'tay Ah Vone!*"

—**Rachel Thompson,** *daughter, author, and eager food eater*

Sandra,
Hope you enjoy my stories and recipes.
Fondly,
Linda

In the Kitchen With Linda

Loving Memories, Favorite Recipes, and Handy Hints

Linda Carsman

Published by
Munn Avenue Press
300 Main Street, Ste 21
Madison, NJ 07940
Munn Avenue Press

E-book ISBN: 978-1-940206-00-4
Paperback ISBN: 978-1-960299-40-6
Hardcover ISBN: 978-1-960299-41-3

Cover Design by Jerboa Design Studio
Cover Image via Shutterstock (ID #2080062649). Used with permission.
Food photographs © 2024 by Linda Carsman
Family photographs from author's private collection © 2024 by Linda Carsman
Author photograph © 2018 by Kimberly S. Olker, of Olker Photography

This memoir-cookbook is dedicated to the loves of my life:

My husband, Jerry, of 65 years and still going strong, who has never complained about any meal I've ever served him.... I told him, I would love him "till the Twelfth of Never," and that's a very long time.

To my daughters, Caren, Rachel, and Leslie: My beautiful, talented, loving, and amazing women who make the world a better place. I love and am so proud of all of you.

To my grandchildren, Sarah, Anya, Lukas, Micah, Hannah, Elijah, and great-granddaughter Lael: Each time one of you was born, my heart grew bigger and bigger with my love for all of you. It's been my blessing to be your "Bammy."

And to my dear friend Marion, who came into my life, almost 70 years ago, as a friend of the heart.

Table of Contents

RECIPES

Appetizers, Noodle Kugel, and Blintzes

Soups

Salads

Fruits

Breakfast

Lunch

Vegetables

Meats, Seafood, and Mains

Meats

Desserts

Typical (or not) Holiday Meals

A Jewish Home

Growing up in a Jewish home with two Eastern European (Ashkenazi) parents, I always knew we were Jewish and somehow different, but it was a home filled with love and always with good food.

My mom Freda (Bamma) met my dad Leonard (Poppy), shortly after my birth-father died while my mom was on a trip to Miami Beach. She was staying with a friend, and Dad was living next door in a duplex unit, having just been discharged from the Army/Air Force. Dad was a Florida resident, originally from the Bronx, NY, who had moved to Florida as a young man in search of a place where his asthma could be better controlled.

Linda's Parents: Freda and Leonard Harris

Mom had lived her entire life in the Flatbush section of Brooklyn, where being Jewish was like breathing. Her family were not religious but were cultural and very family-oriented Jews. She kept kosher because it was the proper thing to do until, as I mention elsewhere, I was a terrible eater: before someone gave me bacon and awakened my taste buds.

Mom and Dad met in Miami Beach, courted the month of February, and decided to get married in June. She came home to me — I'd been staying with my aunts and grandparents while she was away — and announced she was getting married in June, and we were moving to Florida. She never talked much about it; however, I don't imagine her family was very supportive of her decision initially because they didn't know him. Marry they did, in Brooklyn, on June 16, 1946, when I was five and a half years old. We flew to Florida (my first plane ride), and they bought a little house in Boca Raton, a small town, at that time, of 250 families. Theirs turned out to be a beautiful love story that lasted until Dad died, way too young, on the morning of the first Passover *Seder,* April 6, 1974.

Linda's Grandparents: Jacob and Clara Reich

Dad was a wonderful man who loved me as though I were his child, and I was. To me, he was one of the angels who walked the earth. He adopted me and changed my last name from Cohen to Harris. He was outgoing, friendly, positive, and giving; within a short time, he knew almost everybody in Boca Raton. He joined the volunteer fire department, and because he was a World War II veteran, he was able to get a government job working for the Boca Raton Post Office. He joined the American

Legion, Veterans of Foreign Wars, the local Lions Club, and was already a member of the Elks Lodge in Miami Beach, so it was, for him, a very busy and active life.

There was one other Jewish couple in town, and Dad met them early on. South Florida was very prejudiced against Jews and against the Black community, but my dad was loved by all who met him. He barbecued for local churches at their picnic days, he sang in their shows (having a beautiful tenor voice), he marched in the veterans' parades, and, of course, he knew everyone from the post office where all mail was either general delivery or rented mailboxes.

He was revered in the Black community also. He would read and write return letters for those in that community who couldn't read or write, especially those whose sons were incarcerated at Rayford Prison. Dad would deliver mail on his own time to the folks who lived in Pearl City, the Black community north of Boca Raton, if he knew they couldn't come to the post office. (As a funny aside: years later, as Boca Raton grew up and around Pearl City, those properties became very valuable to land developers, and the folks who owned those little homes became very wealthy. Sweet justice!)

My mom had a harder time adjusting to life in a non-Jewish, very small town. My brother, Jonathan, was born 13 months after they married, and she was busy with a baby and a six-year-old. She cooked and she baked a lot and soon became famous for her cakes at school and at organization cake sales. People would bid on her cakes way above anyone else's.

Though being a housewife and mother filled her days, she also became a member of the community. She joined the Auxiliaries of Dad's clubs; took over the kitchen of my local four-room schoolhouse and cooked lunch meals for a few years; joined a committee of the Palm Beach County School Board, which was an appointed position at that time; and met lovely people, one of whom was a widow, Nicki Wilson, who had been married to a Jewish man. (Nicki gave Mom a series of four artist's proofs, hand-signed, of Eastern European Jewish elders celebrating *Shabbat.* Nicki was not Jewish, but she wanted her husband's pictures to go into a Jewish home. They are now well-known pictures in the art world. Mom gave them to me, and now they're hanging in our daughter Caren's home.)

My mom was an excellent bridge player and became known among the "snowbirds" (people who came to Boca Raton for the winter) as the local to join them. Boca Raton was a town of working people who lived there year-round and of the very wealthy who came for the winter. The Boca Raton Hotel was the playground for the affluent and was owned by a Jewish family. When Hildegard Schein, wife of the owner, was in town, Mom had a regular bridge game in the owner's suite of the hotel where she was wined and dined. She kept her ability to play the game most of her life. I'm sorry I never thought to ask her where and how she learned.

What the Moon Brought, by Sadie Rose Weilerstein

Anyway, back to being Jewish in South Florida in the late 1940s-early 1950s. There was no temple or synagogue locally for us to attend, so Dad bought me two books about being Jewish. One was about the Jewish forefathers and mothers, the heroes and the stories of the Old Testament; and the other was about the Jewish holidays, titled *What the Moon Brought*, by Sadie Rose Weilerstein. This is how I learned my basic Judaism.

Then into town for the winter came a lady from Bath, Maine: Estelle Smith, a member of the Orkin family of pest control fame. Dad, of course, met her at the post office, and she became my first teacher of Judaism. I rode my bike to her home every week for my lessons when she was in town. She was a retired educator and very knowledgeable about Judaism.

When I was in the fourth grade, we joined Temple Emanu-El in Ft. Lauderdale, Florida, and went to *Shabbat* services every Friday night. It was about a 50-mile round trip, and Dad drove me back there on Sunday mornings for religious school. Before joining this Temple, there was no organized religion in our house. Mom made a big dinner with matzo balls and soup, chopped liver and brisket for Passover, but we didn't celebrate it with a *Seder.* It was just a special dinner, and the house was always crowded.

Then in 1956, when Jon was 9 and I was 15, we moved to Rialto, California (San Bernardino area) and joined Temple Emanu-El on North "E" Street in San Bernardino. Two and a half years later, Jerry and I met. His Aunt Ruth Trachtenberg sang in the Temple Emanu-El choir, as did my dad's sister, my Aunt Anna (her last name was Walt). Aunt Anna lived with her daughter and son-in-law, Eleanor and Hy Weinstein, who were both federal government employees at Norton AFB in San Bernardino. Aunt Anna was my dad's (Leonard Harris) oldest sister. She lived with her parents along with her daughter, Eleanor, in Forest Hills, Flushing, NY, and she took care of her parents as they got older. Eleanor was only a few years younger than my dad since Aunt Anna was the oldest in the family and dad was the youngest son of six children.

Linda and Jerry, Wedding Day

When Aunt Anna's and dad's mother, Rachel Harris, died, Anna moved to California to live with her daughter Eleanor and son-in-law Hy. Aunt Anna had a lovely singing voice and joined the Temple choir, where she met Aunt Ruth Trachtenberg, and they became friends. When we moved to Rialto, my mom and dad met Ruth and Jack Trachtenberg through Aunt Anna. Then Ruth introduced my parents to her brother and sister-in-law, Morrie and Adele Carsman. And they became friends.

Aunt Ruth met me and, knowing she had a lovely nephew, schemed for the two of us to meet. She was our matchmaker. It took until January of 1958 — two years after my parents joined the Temple — for Jerry and me to meet at a "family gathering" at his parents' house, where we listened to music in Jerry's room, at a very high volume, with his Klipschorn speakers taking up half the room. He introduced me to Gustav Holtz's *The Planets*, drove me home that night, asked me out for the following weekend when we went to the movies and saw *Raintree County.* (And the rest, as they say, is history.)

My husband, Jerry, grew up in an Eastern-European Jewish family also, but in Chicago. His parents were from Pennsylvania, but he was born in Detroit. They moved to Chicago when he was three and then to California when he was eleven. They were not religious at all, but his mother (Adele) and her mother (Grandma Fern) made gefilte fish from scratch since white fish and pike were readily available from Chicago's Jewish fishmongers. That's about all that he remembers from his Jewish childhood. He did have a *Bar Mitzvah,* where not a single photo was taken, but his parents hosted a party in their backyard that made the little Muscoy neighborhood newspaper, with the headline, "Jerry Carsman Honored on Thirteenth Birthday." It was just after World War II, and they were afraid to be known as Jewish.

Jerry Carsman Honored on Thirteenth Birthday

Mr. and Mrs. Morris Carsman, honored their son Jerry's thirteenth birthday, Sunday July 9th by holding open house from 3 to 6 p.m.

Jerry assisted his father as host, and greeted friends and relatives with gracious dignity.

Mr. and Mrs. Harry Frank, maternal grandparents of Jerry assisted Mrs. Carsman in welcoming their many friends and members of the family.

A bountiful buffet supper was served, climaxed by the cutting of an immense and beautiful birthday cake.

Mr. Brownfield took moving pictures to record this eventful day for Jerry and his family.

Jerry's 13th Birthday Announcement

As a teenager, through the temple, Jerry joined Aleph Zadik Aleph (AZA) and made Jewish friends; since fourth grade, his best friend has been Steve Klein. Marion, who later became Steve's wife, as well as a lifetime friend of mine, was two years younger than Jerry and Steve, and Jerry knew her from dual teenage AZA/BBG (B'nai B'rith Girls) events.

Grandma Adele had grown more comfortable within the temple family after they left Muscoy (a rural area of San Bernardino) and moved into San Bernardino proper, just a few blocks away, within walking distance from the temple. She made Jewish friends and joined the weekly bulletin-folding crew, which she did for many, many years.

Not one of my finest moments but I remember, at a Passover *Seder,* at our house, lashing out at Grandma Adele after she belittled us for teaching the prayers and story of the *Seder* to my daughters — her grandchildren — Caren and Rachel. I think it was the first time I ever responded to her without my being all sweetness and light. In retrospect, looking back and learning about her life and how she was raised, I've grown to understand where her bitterness and sharpness came from. She was of the generation where girls were not valued, and she and her sister, Aunt June, grew up feeling unloved and unwanted.

Jerry's Parents: Adele and Morrie Carsman

When Adele was thirteen and June was ten, Jerry's Grandma Fern and Grandpa Harry (Zadie) had another baby — and unto them, a Jewish prince was born: Uncle Bobby, who was 10 years older than Jerry. Then Adele and Morrie had two sons, and Aunt June had three sons, so between them, five grandsons. As daughters who gave them grandsons, they became more valued.

Jerry's Grandparents:Fern and Harry Frank

Adele told me, when I was pregnant with Caren, that the Carsmans only had sons, so I wrote "think pink" cards and placed them all over our apartment. Obviously, my signs worked. I know she grew to love and appreciate her granddaughters, but — may she rest in peace — she was a difficult mother and mother-in-law. However, she raised Jerry to the best of her ability, and he's a wonderful husband, father, and grandfather, so I'm grateful to her for that.

So many of the foods and recipes included here are what I remember eating at Jewish holidays. I have not separated them into their own chapters but have included them within the food categories where they belong. This I have done intentionally to keep you turning through the pages of this little book of love; however, you'll find whatever foods you're looking for. I tried to include everyone's favorites along with recipes that I didn't want to get lost through the ages.

Linda and Jerry Carsman: 60th Wedding Anniversary

Restaurants

Once in a while, I need a break from cooking, so restaurants, here we come!

From our very first dates, Jerry and I loved going to restaurants. His favorites in San Bernardino were The Mug for pizza, and Pail of Chicken for fried chicken and fried shrimp. The Mug was famous for its cheese pizza, which was cut crosswise across the middle and then into strips.

He ate out a lot as a young man because Grandma Adele worked at their liquor store, and he didn't want to go home after school and then work at the store: so he had to fend for himself. She'd make a lot of stewed meats and pot roasts that she could leave for Jerry and his brother Mel, but once Jerry got a car, he was hardly at home.

He did his homework at Ruby's Drive In, sitting in his car with the lights as his illumination. He also loved the Orange Julius in downtown San Bernardino for their orange drink and their chili cheese hot dogs that they smothered in Parmesan cheese and toasted until crisp.

And then there was Queens for the best sub sandwiches ever served. Their bread was delicious and made fresh for them at a local bakery: crunchy yet soft and not too "bready." He got ham and cheese along with everything the sandwiches came with: thin sliced tomatoes, shredded lettuce, and thin sliced onion that had been marinated in a delicious oil and vinegar dressing. Queens became a favorite for all of our years in San Bernardino.

When we were dating, a favorite stop after a movie date was a Chinese restaurant called Bing's on Highland Avenue. We'd get egg rolls, fried rice, and their best dish, Almond Pressed Duck. It was delicious: crisp duck strips, pressed thin, served with a sweet sauce, and topped with chopped toasted almonds on a bed of shredded lettuce. So good (and apparently so time-consuming that very few Chinese restaurants make it anymore. I found a description, and recipe, of it online, and the recipe will make you salivate for it).

For very special occasions, we drove to Cucamonga to one of two restaurants, almost across the street from each other: The Magic Lamp and The Sycamore Inn. 65 years later, they're both still in business. Our granddaughter Sarah and her family lived in Rancho Cucamonga from 2017-2021, and verified both restaurants are still in operation.

The Sycamore Inn was more expensive, and I only recall going there once or twice. The Magic Lamp was famous for their large baked potatoes, grilled meats, and their famous side that came with every entree: a huge serving of stuffing covered with a turkey gravy. Every meal came with toasted cheese bread and a crisp salad. Crazy combination of foods but, oh, so good. It's a wonder that we survived eating like that, but it was not often, maybe twice a year. We ate there in 1958 when dating and maybe a few times in 1959 as newlyweds.

When we moved to Los Angeles in 1960, Jerry worked in the liquor department at the Hollywood Ranch Market on the three-to-midnight shift. We ate lunches (not dinners) out on his day off, and our favorite, of course, was Canter's Deli on Fairfax near Melrose. Aunt Ruthie Carsman and her husband Uncle David lived walking distance to Canter's, and their dry cleaning store was also walking distance on Spaulding and Melrose. We'd stop to say "hello" to Aunt Ruthie and her mom, Mrs. Levy, who sat in the front window of the store, repairing clothes on her manually operated sewing machine. Oh, the memories.

Canter's was our favorite spot. We'd get bean and barley soup, corned beef and pastrami sandwiches, coleslaw, new pickles, and then make a stop in their attached bakery, which was a show unto itself. Take a number, wait your turn, and then yell out your order over the din of the other customers. It was a fun happening.

The waitstaff, at that time, were all older women who wore crisp yellow uniforms with large starched, beautiful handkerchiefs attached by pins to their shoulders. The gimmick of Canter's staff was the way they greeted you at the table: "What'da you want?" "Hurry up. I don't have all day." It was part of the *schtick:* they were lovely ladies who took good care of us. And the food was always consistent and so good.

When we visited Caren, Chris, and Sarah in Bakersfield, we always had great meals in their restaurants: I've referenced Momma Tosca's for the carrots. The best Mexican food I've ever eaten has to have been at El Pueblo in Lamont. Their Cancun shrimp was so delicious, and it introduced us to Mexican-style seafood. (I think I'm going to try to reconstruct it: battered fried shrimp served in a lightly spicy sauce reminiscent of chile relleno/green enchilada sauce, sprinkled with cheese, and broiled. Mmmm! That's my recollection, at any rate.) Bakersfield also had great Mediterranean cuisine and amazing Chinese food. I remember eating well in Bakersfield.

We have always had great meals in Napa Valley. Years ago, our favorite was always the restaurant at the Domaine Chandon Winery. Jerry, as the "wine buyer" for a retail drugstore, always got their private winery tours and tastings as a complimentary service. We took many friends and family on these tours where we drank way too much champagne, and then we'd go into the restaurant for a 2–3-hour meal on their back patio. Hopefully, we weren't as inebriated when we left as when we entered. The food was always so good and presented so beautifully. From what I've heard, it's not the same anymore, so this is not a recommendation, just a memory from the mid-1980s.

Also in Napa Valley, in Rutherford, is the Rutherford Grill, right on the main highway. Everything there is delicious, but their French Dip sandwich is amazing. It will spoil you, and you'll always compare every French Dip sandwich, going forward, with Rutherford Grill's. They prepare rotisserie rib roasts to only use for these sandwiches, and you can see them turning over and over on the rotisserie in the back kitchen. And you can smell them. Their fresh vegetables are also delicious. We usually get their red sautéed cabbage as our side with the sandwich.

The next valley over, the Sonoma and Santa Rosa area, is where two of our all-time dining experiences have been. We stay at a timeshare in Windsor and do most of our own cooking. However, dinner at John Ash Restaurant is a must-do reservation, as is lunch and wine tasting at Kendall-Jackson Winery.

John Ash was one of the first California chefs to go "farm to fork." His restaurant is a comfortable, welcoming space, especially in our favorite seating area — the inside/outside dining room — with always interesting dining options and new tastes and flavors from which to choose.

KENDALL-JACKSON

Wine & Food Pairing

2018 Jackson Estate Panorama Vineyard
Rosé of Pinot Noir
Monterey County
Farmer T's Lettuces, Plums, Beets, Radish, Fennel, Chevoo Goat Cheese, Ume Vinagarette

2017 Jackson Estate Fulton Ranch Chardonnay
Russian River Valley, Sonoma County

Wild King Salmon, Horseradish, Little Farm Potato Salad, Summer Squash, Trout Caviar

2015 Jackson Estate Trace Ridge Cabernet Sauvignon
Knights Valley, Sonoma County

Snake River Farms Coulotte Steak, Carrot – Pumpkin Puree, Tokyo Turnip, Tatsoi

2016 Vintner's Reserve Muscat Canelli
California

Vanilla Bean Mousse, Estate Plum Jam, Corn Cake, Candied Marcona Almonds, Plum-Verjus Sorbet

Canelés de Bordeaux

KENDALL-JACKSON WINE ESTATE AND GARDENS

Sample Kendall-Jackson Food & Wine Pairing Menu

We had stuffed squash blossoms here as an appetizer: so good and beyond my culinary skills. Otherwise, if you're not adventurous, fear not: the menu is all-encompassing and has something for everyone.

Kendall-Jackson Winery has the most fabulous food and wine pairing that we've ever tasted. You get 6-7 tastings of wine and full pours, and each is served with a food pairing that's been prepared by their personal chef. He comes out and discusses likes, dislikes, and/or allergies, and then the magic happens. Each course comes out with his explanation of why it was paired and what tastes to expect. Then it ends with a dessert paired with my favorite: a sweet, late harvest Riesling. And as you're leaving, you get your own personal bag of homemade caramel popcorn. We've shared many food and wine pairings: this one at Kendall-Jackson Winery is the best. No matter who we're with or how many times we've been here, it's always a magical experience.

Since the Covid pandemic, we've hardly been out for dinner in restaurants. Although restrictions have been lifted, four years later, we're still not going out to dine very often. An occasional dinner out to celebrate a birthday or an anniversary or with our dining-out group is the extent of our going out. It's been more fun for me to spend time in the kitchen cooking and creating enjoyable meals.

My Thoughts on 65 Years of Cooking

My daughters have asked over the years for some of my recipes, and I set out to collect the scraps of paper many were written on, to find and modernize some of them, and to share stories which recall Bamma Freda, Grandma Adele, and memories of wonderful meals with family and friends. This has turned into a memoir of recipes, my take on restaurant recipes, and fond remembrances of people and fun times throughout the years, starting as a young bride and continuing into the present times.

As far back as I can remember, food has always been important to me; however, according to family lore, I was a terrible eater as a toddler. My mom used to bargain with family members to come and feed me while she did their ironing. (She enjoyed ironing??? Crazy!!!)

My grandmother Clara (my mom's mother) had a much younger brother, Abe, who, along with his wife, Tillie, was more like a contemporary family than like an aunt and uncle to my mom. Aunt Tillie would come over to feed me on a regular basis. Apparently, she told me stories, and I would open my mouth as she stuffed me with food.

The family were all Eastern-European Jews from the area known as the Pale of Settlement, a western region of the Russian Empire. Russian, Lithuanian, and Austrian Jews were from the Pale. (You've heard the phrase, "beyond the Pale"? Russian Jews from the Pale believe that's where it originated.) At the time the family emigrated in the 1890s, their town of Buczacz (pronounced "Boo Chooch") was part of the Austria-Hungarian Empire. It is now part of western Ukraine.

The family was not religious but rather were cultural Jews. It was easy, living in Brooklyn, to be Jewish, and being Jewish meant keeping a kosher household. Butcher shops, delis, corner grocery stores: all were kosher and within walking distance in the neighborhood. Keeping kosher was not difficult. And then, someone, somewhere... gave me bacon, which is not kosher, and apparently, that's where my love story with food began. Bacon came into the house, and I was hooked on food. And my mother didn't keep kosher anymore.

My mother (Freda) never made pork chops or roasts or mixed dairy with meat when I was a child — old habits die hard — but when we moved to Florida in 1946 and settled in Boca Raton, there were no kosher butcher shops, so she learned that non-kosher meats were perfectly safe.

She missed certain foods and seasonings that were only available in Jewish neighborhoods, so about 3-4 times a year, we drove down to Miami Beach, about 40 miles away, and Mom stocked up. This was a very long trip, believe it or not. No freeways, just US Highway 1, driving through every town between Boca and Miami Beach that probably took one and a half to two hours. We visited

Aunt Tillie and Uncle Abe, who lived in one of the little hotels in what is now known as South Beach.

Then we went to Wolfie's Deli to have their corned beef sandwiches. I remember loving the pickles that were brought to the table in large tubs and refilled as needed. It wasn't until years later, in Los Angeles at Canter's Deli, that I discovered pastrami sandwiches. Yum! Yum!

(A funny memory that just got triggered: my dad, who married my mom when I was 5 1/2 years old and who adopted me, had a brother who lived in Miami Beach. My mother liked Uncle Louie but took an instant dislike to his wife, Libby. Dad saw his brother when he went to Miami for business, and Mom was okay with that since she didn't want to socialize with them.

We were at Wolfie's once, and my brother Jonathan, who was probably 4 or 5 years old, had gone outside to play. [Yes, in those days, kids could do that.] Mom went out to check on him and saw him sitting on the hood of a car. She yelled at him to get off the car, and he ignored her, so she moved closer. It wasn't my brother: it was Louie and Libby's son. They were in the same restaurant. Dad went off to find his brother to say "hello" and tell them what had happened, and Mom brought my brother back inside. Years later, at Dad's funeral, Louie came by himself, and I couldn't stop staring at him: he and Dad looked so much alike. And my brother looked like Dad, and Louie's son looked like him, so no wonder Mom mistook Louie's for Jon.)

Mom then learned about Florida seafood and shellfish; and shrimp, crab, and Florida lobster worked their way into her kitchen. But not for me. Those things looked funny to me, and I didn't eat shrimp or lobster until Jerry and I were on our honeymoon. He ordered a shrimp cocktail and gave me a taste, and I was hooked. The presentation was gorgeous, with the red cocktail sauce in a large, stemmed bowl and the shrimp curled around the edges. Oh, my! The things we remember.

My parents were both cooking masters and impressed upon me the need for a clean and orderly kitchen. Clean up after yourself as you go. Wash the utensils, pots and pans, and other implements as you're finished with them; that way, when dinner is over, there's nothing left to clean except the plates and dining utensils. It's much easier now that I usually only cook for two. Unless we have company for dinner, there's nothing left to wash except our two plates and forks and knives.

Speaking of forks, my favorite cooking implement is my dad's World War II mess kit eating fork. He had two of them, and my brother Jon and I each took one when Dad died. We both treasure them and use ours as Dad did: as cooking implements.

It may seem strange, with all the kitchen gadgets available, that Dad's fork is what I use the most when cooking. The handle is flat, smooth, and just fits in the palm of my hand perfectly. I use it to turn foods over when grilling, browning, stirring, mixing, roasting, or whatever else I'm doing in the kitchen. It's the perfect utensil but more than that: it's my connection to my dad even though he's been gone for almost fifty years. (Daddy, your memory lives on through your grandchildren who knew you, Caren and Rachel, and your grandchildren who came along after you died, Leslie, and Jon's children, Ron, and Jenny. Even your great-grandchildren know of you and your stories and memories.) Oh, my, all these

My Dad's World War II Mess Kit Fork

memories and thoughts over a kitchen fork.

We got our first dishwasher in 1976, and with five of us in the family, that dishwasher got a fair workout. It didn't stop the squabbling, however: it just changed from whose turn it was to dry the dishes to whose turn it was to empty the dishwasher.

When we moved to our new home in 1997, it was just the two of us, and dishes would sit in the dishwasher for days until it got full enough to run, so I was rinsing dishes so the dishwasher wouldn't smell. This made no sense to me, so I just started hand-washing our few dishes every night after dinner. Modern conveniences are wonderful, but I've found as I've gotten older, the more things change, the more they stay the same.

My cooking has evolved from dinners for two, to dinners for four and then five as our family grew, and now back to dinners for two again. I've become a stovetop cook: lots of one-meal skillet meals, e.g., stir-fries, grilled steaks and chops, and sautéed vegetables. I have not adapted to solely cooking for two, however. My new mantra is "Cook once, eat twice." And so, we do.

I've never considered myself to be a gourmet cook but just a great cook who made delicious family meals. I learned to cook after Jerry and I got married, using, at the beginning, the Betty Crocker cookbook we received as a wedding gift. I didn't even know how to crack open an egg when we got married. My brother Jon, who was about 11, and who had learned in Boy Scout camp, taught me how to crack open an egg.

Other than a few holiday recipes, my mom didn't teach me how to cook. She didn't know how to teach: she just did. Years later, I learned cabbage soup and brisket from watching her, stopping her and measuring what she did as she went along. Then I adapted her recipes to our tastes.

Some of my best cooking tips were learned from our friend Marion. She is an excellent cook, and we spent a lot of time together after we moved back to San Bernardino in 1965. She and her husband Steve, who was Jerry's best friend and best man at our wedding, had just moved into a big, beautiful home with a great kitchen; our home, which was our first home, was very small. We cooked and ate at their house. My girls Caren and Rachel will tell you that we ate steak and fed them hamburgers, and I guess we sometimes did when budgets were tight, but mostly they ate what we did.

We did pick up Chinese food a lot from Wong's Kitchen: a take-out, hole-in-the-wall kitchen that we thought was delicious but that, in retrospect, was pretty bad. It was fresh food, however, as opposed to the Chun King in-the-can food that served as the introduction to Chinese food in the 1950s and 1960s.

Marion and I once made a recipe from Chef Mike Roy of KNX Radio in Los Angeles. It was a prime rib roast smothered in kosher salt and roasted. It wasn't supposed to be salty to eat: the salt coating was to keep the juices in and keep it tender. It didn't, and it wasn't. We had to chisel the baked-on salt off to get to the meat, which was just awful. And we could ill afford what the roast cost us. We did not dine well that night.

Another time we made *kreplach* (Jewish dumplings) from scratch. We made the dough, cooked and ground the beef and onions for the filling, and then cooked the filled dumplings in the pot of chicken broth we'd made. It took hours, and when they were finally finished, we tasted them. They were delicious, and we kept stuffing our faces until we realized there were only a dozen left. Those we served to Jerry and Steve. The kids got soup, rice, and shredded chicken. And we never made *kreplach* again.

We also became, in our minds, sophisticated wine connoisseurs. Jerry would bring home

Mateus wine for our red, and Blue Nun for our white, and from those humble beginnings, we really learned about wine and food pairing. We made regular trips to Napa Valley, took wine tours, met with winemakers, and really did become pretty discriminating wine enthusiasts.

(Jerry became the "wine buyer" for a northern California retail drugstore, and that gave us opportunities for private tours and tastings. The wineries thought he was the buyer for the entire chain, and, in a way, he was. He had the largest and best wine cage in any of the chain's drugstores, and the company executives, including the CEO himself, used to drive in from the Bay Area to purchase wine from Jerry's store.)

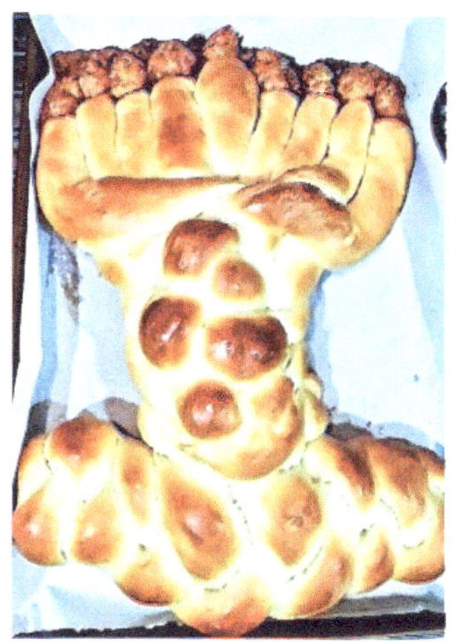

Leslie's Chanukah Challah

Some favorite recipes have been passed down from my mother, usually soups and holiday meals; she always made delicious cakes, which I do not do. I'm a cook, not a baker. Granddaughter Sarah is a wonderful cook, as is her husband Chris, and they're passing that talent down to their daughter, our great-granddaughter, Lael, already a talented, budding little chef.

Although baking is a gene that I think is passed through the generations, it definitely skipped me. I can salvage almost anything cooked: "a little of this, a little of that," and something tasty can always be served. The more experience you have cooking, the easier it gets. I learned that since I don't cook chicken anymore (it's a food intolerance), I can substitute shrimp, beef, or pork and still serve a delicious meal. Combining our food tastes along with what's in the pantry gets easier and easier with experience. Use leftovers to your advantage: make chicken chili if you've got leftover chicken; use leftover pork chops or roast in a pot of soup or a stir fry; make green "chicken" enchiladas using cut-up and sautéed shrimp. It all works: just cook, and your confidence in the kitchen will grow.

Not so with baking! Baking requires patience and following the science of measuring and calculating ingredients. Baking is just not me; however, I take joy in watching my daughter Leslie and granddaughter Anya bake and enjoy themselves. It is a talent. It's so much fun for me to watch Leslie make challah for her family. She whips up the dough, lets it rise, punches it down, lets it rise again, rolls it out, fills it, braids and shapes, and bakes it. I get tired watching her, but she loves it. I must admit, she makes a delicious challah, and I do enjoy eating it. She reminds me of the story of the Little Red Hen, except Leslie makes her challah with love and happily shares.

And so it is, 65 years of *In the Kitchen with Linda*. Now for some recipes...

Appetizers, Kugel, and Blintzes

I'm not big on serving appetizers, but occasionally they're requested, so here are my favorites.

Come to think of it, for someone who said she doesn't do appetizers, it seems like I really do like them, considering how many recipes I have for them.

Maybe the answer is to not have dinners but to just do appetizers. Add the "Sticky Chicken" recipe from the "Meats" section, and some of the above suggestions would make a great party.
B'tay Ah Vone!

Holiday Veggie Dip

Try it: you'll love it. Just don't call it "chopped liver."

My mother made the most delicious chopped chicken liver (if you like liver, which I don't), and she was famous for hers. I used to sneak the onions she sautéed but wouldn't eat the finished product; Jerry, on the other hand, loved it. So, when I came across this recipe for "Mock Chopped Liver," I gave it a try, and it was just so good that it became a favorite, but it needed a name change. Now it's called "Holiday Veggie Dip," and it's served with matzo for Passover and crackers at other times.

Even the chopped liver addicts will love it.

---

1 can Le Sueur peas, drained

3 onions chopped: about 3 cups, finely chopped, with ½ cup reserved and remaining uncooked

2 hard-boiled eggs, peeled, cooled, and chopped

⅔ cup toasted walnuts, chopped (see Note)

¼ cup vegetable oil

Heat the oil and sauté and caramelize 2 ½ cups of the onion until dark brown but not burned, 25-30 minutes on low. Cool to room temperature.

Mash the canned peas with a fork into a paste.

In a large bowl, place cooked onion, oil, chopped eggs, peas, raw onion, and walnuts. Combine well; season with salt and pepper to taste.

Refrigerate until completely chilled and ready to serve.

Serve with crackers or matzos.

Bamma Freda's Chopped Chicken Liver

For real chopped liver lovers, I found my mom's recipe that she contributed to a synagogue cookbook, so here it is, as it was written, circa 1958.

2 onions, medium-sized, chopped
¼ cup oil
Chicken livers, one pound
2 hard-boiled eggs, peeled, cooled, and chopped

Heat the oil, and sauté, stirring often, the onions, for 15 minutes. Remove onions to wooden chopping bowl.

In same pan, add more oil, as needed, and sauté washed and drained chicken livers until light brown and cooked through.

Cool chicken livers at room temperature until you can handle them. Then chop very fine, in wooden bowl, the livers, onions, and hard-boiled eggs. Season with salt and pepper to taste.

Chill in the refrigerator until time to serve.

Serve as a spread on crackers or matzos, or on a lettuce leaf for salad or appetizers.

Mini Wrapped Hotdogs

There's not much of a recipe here — just buy biscuit dough and mini hotdogs and the big secret: sweet and hot mustard.

Mini hot dogs, any brand
2 tubes large biscuits (8 biscuits each)
Sweet and hot mustard

Cut biscuits into thirds, about 48 pieces. Stretch biscuit pieces with your hands and tightly roll a hot dog into each one. Place on a sheet pan, seam side down, and press until flat.

Bake according to biscuit directions and serve with sweet and hot (or any other choice) mustard.

Note: Make twice as many as you think you'll need because even the "healthy food" eaters will gobble these down.

Sweet and Sour Meatballs

We had these at a party shortly after we got married.

These were a very popular recipe in the early 1960s and are so simple to make. They didn't have ready-made frozen meatballs then, but now they're available, and that's a perfect shortcut for this recipe.

One jar grape jelly
One jar cocktail sauce
One package frozen, fully cooked meatballs

Combine grape jelly and cocktail sauce in saucepan. Cook on low-to-medium heat, and stir until jelly melts and combines well with cocktail sauce.

Add meatballs and cook on low-to-medium heat until meatballs are warmed through, about 20 minutes.

Serve with toothpicks. They are yummy.

Bubbie's Meatballs

These were served at my friend's house for all Jewish holiday meals.

I'm also going to include another meatball recipe for "holiday meatballs appetizer" that a friend's mother taught me. This one is a little more work but definitely worth it because they're delicious. She had nothing written down, so I watched her and stopped her as she did each step; we measured everything as she did it, and these are the delicious results.

Sauce:

One 8-ounce can tomato sauce
½ onion, chopped fine
Pinch of sugar
Pinch of salt
½ teaspoon oil

Combine all ingredients in a saucepan, cover, and simmer until onions get soft, about the time it takes to make the meatballs.

Meatballs:

1 slice white bread, soaked in water and squeezed dry
1 egg, beaten and mixed with bread
1 pound lean ground beef
Squeeze of lemon juice
1 tablespoon sugar
½ onion, chopped very fine
⅓ cup ketchup
⅓ cup brown sugar

Sear meatballs in hot pan until browned and then transfer into pot with sauce. Cook slowly for 20-25 minutes.

Add ketchup and brown sugar. Cook another 15 minutes.

Serve as a holiday appetizer.

Caren's Meatballs

I love meatballs, and this recipe is from my daughter, Caren, who learned it from a friend.

Meatballs are a favorite of mine, and these are easy and so delicious.

One 26-ounce package of frozen meatballs
One 12-ounce jar of Heinz Savory Beef Gravy (see Note)
6 ounces sour cream, full fat or low-fat

Mix gravy and sour cream together and place in a slow cooker. Add meatballs and cook on high for one hour, then reduce heat to low and cook for another 3 hours.

Serve from the slow cooker. Easy, simple, and so good.

Caren's Meatballs

Momma Tosca's Copycat Marinated Carrots

I can't remember my main course that night, but I sure can't forget these delicious carrots.

When Caren and Chris lived in Bakersfield, they took us to an Italian restaurant called Momma Tosca's, where they served the most delicious cold garlicky carrots as an appetizer. Of course, I had to go home and try to recreate it. Here's my take on their carrot appetizer.

These are so good, make a lot of them. Portions are my guesstimates, so add more oil or vinegar as needed.

2 pounds of carrots, peeled and sliced into rounds
6 tablespoons olive oil
6 tablespoons balsamic vinegar
2-3 cloves chopped garlic
Salt and pepper to taste

Put carrots in pot and cover with water. Bring to a boil. Lower heat and cook on low until carrots are tender. Drain carrots and transfer to a bowl.

Add olive oil, balsamic vinegar, chopped garlic, and salt and pepper. Refrigerate and let marinate for 24 hours, stirring occasionally.

Taste and adjust seasonings.

Serve on an antipasto platter or by themselves. Delish!!!

Baked Olives

Olives are not my favorite, but I tasted these, and they were amazing.

The previous recipe reminded me of the fabulous baked olives we were served at a Napa Valley restaurant. I don't like olives, but these were amazing, so again, my take on how good olives can be.

Note: don't use canned black or green pimento olives (also known as Spanish Olives or Spanish Stuffed Olives) for this recipe.

1 jar Mezzetta Italian Castelvetrano Olives, whole or pitted, drained

1 pound assorted olives from a specialty grocer with an olive bar, including, for instance Niçoise, Kalamata, and/or Picholine olives

Italian seasoning, to taste (see Note)

Garlic, to taste

Zest of one lemon

Olive oil, ½ cup

Balsamic vinegar, ¼-½ cup

Peel of an orange cut into pieces

Salt and pepper to taste

Season olives with Italian seasoning, salt and pepper, garlic, and lemon zest. Add olive oil, balsamic vinegar, and the pieces of orange peel. Marinate, in the refrigerator, for 24 hours.

Preheat oven to 350º F.

Transfer olive mixture to baking dish and bake for 20-25 minutes.

Place in a serving dish and watch them disappear.

Antipasto Platter

I have a special flower-printed metal tray that I use for antipasto, and it makes a beautiful presentation. I still have it.

This recipe is one of my old standbys. Years ago, I prepared a large antipasto platter for a dinner party. There's not much cooking involved other than the marinated carrots, but there are lots of tidbits to stimulate the appetite.

Italian salami, cubed, sliced, or whole: your preference
Marinated carrots (recipe here)
Marinated artichoke hearts (any brand)
Havarti cheese, cubed, sliced, or a wedge
Mozzarella cheese, cubed, seasoned or plain
Crackers, assorted
Olives, assorted, such as Kalamata, Castelvetrano, Niçoise, etc.
Cherry tomatoes
Cucumber slices

Arrange all ingredients on a large tray.

Add any other popular antipasto ingredients you'd like, such as prosciutto, pepperoni, gorgonzola, asiago, parmesan, crostini or flatbread, marinated mushrooms, roasted tomatoes, roasted or marinated red peppers, figs or fig jam, etc.

Guaranteed to be a successful party starter.

Linda's Antipasto Platter

Noodle Kugel

This is the best noodle kugel I have ever eaten.

This Noodle Kugel is a holiday food. Our friend Sherry Raffin always made it at our Yom Kippur Break the Fast potlucks, and it must be shared. If by chance you have leftovers, it's delicious cold or reheated.

Topping:

1 cup cornflake crumbs

2 tablespoons sugar

2 tablespoons butter

Melt the butter, and then mix in sugar and cornflake crumbs.

Kugel:

One 12-ounce bag wide noodles

5 eggs, beaten

1 pint (16 ounces) sour cream

8 ounces cream cheese, softened

1 stick (8 tablespoons / ½ cup) butter, softened

1 cup cottage cheese

2 cups Half-and-Half

1 cup sugar

1 teaspoon vanilla

Preheat oven to 350º F.

Cook noodles, drain, and set aside.

Blend together softened butter and softened cream cheese.

In separate bowl, combine sour cream and cottage cheese.

Combine the bowl of blended butter and cream cheese with the bowl of sour cream and cottage cheese. Add eggs, Half-and-Half, sugar, and vanilla. Mix in cooked noodles and stir until noodles are well coated.

Pour into greased lasagna pan (larger than 9x13"). Bake at 350º F for 1 hour or until set in the center, and browned.

Remove kugel when done and spoon topping over noodles. Return to oven and bake 15 minutes longer until the topping starts browning.

Let sit 15 minutes before cutting, or serve at room temperature if taking to a potluck gathering.

It's very rich so cut into 2x2" squares and make 15-20 people very happy. Stand back so you don't get trampled as everyone heads for the food table. Just kidding, but it really is that good.

Blintzes

Time-consuming to make, but a very special treat.

I've included blintzes after the kugel because I remember them as a Break the Fast Yom Kippur food. I think blintzes are also served on Shavuot, the holiday we celebrate to commemorate Moses and the Ten Commandments. Dairy foods are traditionally served along with fruits and nuts.

My mother made the best blintzes that I've ever eaten. She did not make a sweet cheese filling: she used Farmer Cheese which seems to be an East Coast product. She would buy it by the pound as a large, flat (maybe about an inch thick) brick of white cheese. The closest thing is probably dry curd cottage cheese. I have no idea what she added to make the filling, but it was tasty and creamy and delicious but not sweet.

Watching my mom make the crepes for the blintzes was a thing of beauty. Our house had a huge, angled countertop upon which she would lay out a white sheet, then make each crepe in a small frying pan with a flick of her wrist and turn each one out, upside down on the sheet. One after the other until she had made three dozen. They were only cooked on one side with the cooked side facing up. Then she'd fill each one with the farmer or cottage cheese mixture, fold and roll them and refrigerate them covered until ready to fry and serve.

They were so good; I liked jelly with mine, but they were so tasty with just the browned butter that she cooked them in. I have never made blintzes, but I've heard that frozen ones from the grocery store are very good.

Blintz soufflés using frozen blintzes used to be a popular way to serve blintzes without all the work of making and pan-frying them. There are lots of recipes on the Internet for blintzes: making them from scratch, buying frozen and preparing and serving them per the directions, and turning them into a soufflé or casserole when feeding a crowd.

Most blintzes seem to have sweet cheese filling, but I prefer them savory since that's the way my mom made them.

Soups

When the weather turns cool, I think, "soup."

There's nothing like a hot bowl of soup to chase the chills away. I've discovered over the years that I like chopping vegetables, whether for soup or stews or even stir fries. There's something very satisfying about chopping and making piles of them all over my cutting board. Some soups are easy and don't need recipes, others need a helping hand for the proper proportion of ingredients, but all are delicious. I don't cook "spicy," but a few pepper flakes added to some soups are what is needed to amp up the flavors.

Chicken Soup

My earliest food memory is of my grandmother cleaning and cutting up a whole kosher chicken and cooking the unshelled egg yolks in her soup and feeding them to me.

My mother bought a whole chicken, cut it up herself, and made her chicken soup. She then shredded the white meat into the soup and served it with the cooked carrots, onion, parsnips, and celery. She cooked noodles separately to serve with it, or rice if someone was sick, and it was a complete and filling meal. Then she and my dad ate the rest of the boiled chicken sprinkled with salt. Yuk! Not very appealing, but nothing went to waste in the late 1940s-1950s.

Anything left over was turned into chicken salad: chopped up with celery, onion, and mayonnaise. Delicious, and I still make chicken salad with leftover Costco chicken for Jerry. But back to chicken soup, my way.

I use two 32-ounce boxes of chicken broth or stock and add the carrots, celery, onion, and one chicken leg and one thigh that I freeze from the Costco chicken. The "magic" ingredient — taught to me by Elinor Meisinger, my friend Marion's mother — is a tablespoon of ketchup. This gives the soup a little color, richness, and wonderful flavor.

I generally only make chicken soup a couple of times a year; it's not Rosh Hashanah without chicken soup and matzo balls, and again, of course, for Passover. Make your chicken soup however you like, but add that spoonful of ketchup. Try it: you'll like it.

Matzoh Balls and Chicken Soup

Matzo Balls

I tried many times to make matzo balls from scratch, and never achieved "floaters."

Just a thought about matzo balls:

Buy the Manischewitz (or Streit's) boxes, in the Kosher section, with two packages of matzo ball mix in each box. Follow the directions totally and carefully, and you'll have successful "floaters" every time.

Sometimes the matzo ball mix box comes with one package of matzo ball mix and one packet of soup mix. If that's what the store carries, it's perfectly fine. Add carrots, celery, onion, and the required amount of water, and make your soup from that soup mix. Add the spoonful of ketchup: it really does make a difference.

Cooking the matzo balls in the soup instead of just in water gives them a lot of added flavor, but it does make the soup cloudy-looking. I personally like serving chicken soup that's clear, but I must admit that the matzo balls are definitely more flavorful when cooked in the soup.

Another very important factor in making matzo balls: the water or soup must be heavily boiling when the rolled matzo balls are placed in the pot. After the balls are all in, turn down the pot to a continuous lower boil but not a simmer: they must boil to get cooked all the way through. And no peeking during the 20–25-minute cooking process.

Gluten-free matzo ball mix recipes can be found on the net; however, boxed GF matzo ball mix is also available and just as good and easy to make as the original.

Matzo Balls, Cooking

Pasta e Fagioli Soup

The first time I had this soup, a new world of soup-eating opened up for me.

We love this soup at Olive Garden, and I figured out my own version of it. Theirs has a touch of spice which I leave out but add a few pepper flakes if you like spicy. This is almost like a chili but a little soupier.

One 32-ounce box of broth: chicken, beef, or vegetable, your preference
1 pound lean ground beef
½ pound Italian sausage (mild or spicy, to your taste)
1 large can Italian tomatoes, preferably San Marzano style, broken up in the can
1 can white beans, such as cannellini
1 can kidney beans
2 carrots, peeled and chopped
2 celery ribs, chopped
½ large onion, chopped
Salt, pepper, garlic powder, and Italian seasoning (see Note) to taste
Pepper flakes, optional
½ cup Ditalini pasta, cooked separately, and drained
Parmesan cheese for serving

Brown meats in large stockpot and season lightly with salt, pepper, garlic powder, and Italian seasoning. Drain fat and remove meat from pot.

Add carrots, celery, and onion to pot, season lightly and sauté in a little olive oil.

Return the meats to the pot and stir to blend with the vegetables. Add broth, can of tomatoes, and the cans of beans with their liquid. Stir to combine and cook on low, stirring occasionally, for ½ hour.

Add optional pepper flakes, if desired. Taste and season if needed.

Cook Ditalini pasta, drain, and set aside.

When serving, add pasta to soup bowl, ladle in soup, and top with Parmesan cheese.

Momma's Sweet and Sour Cabbage Soup

Everyone who has tasted this soup has asked for the recipe.

My mom was famous for her cabbage soup, an Eastern European way of feeding the family on very little money. She followed no recipe: just chopped cabbage and onion, a tough beef cut (flanken), and whatever canned tomatoes she had on hand. The magic ingredients were brown sugar and sour salt (citric acid), which is not an easy product to find. Freshly squeezed lemon juice works instead of sour salt. Depending on taste preferences, my mom threw in more sugar or more sour salt. One day I watched my mom, took notes, measured everything she did, and came up with my version that Jerry says is delicious. Caren, Rachel, and Leslie give their approval, as does granddaughter, Hannah.

1 head of green cabbage, roughly chopped
2 large onions, chopped
1 large can tomatoes, preferably San Marzano style, broken up in can
1 can tomato paste, optional (see Note)
1 can tomato sauce, optional (see Note)
2 pounds beef, cut into pieces
Beef bouillon, optional (see Note)
Brown sugar
Sour salt (citric acid) (see Note)

Brown and season the meat, with salt and pepper, in a little oil in a stockpot. This gives an extra layer of flavor. Remove meat, retaining the juices in the pot, and set aside the meat.

In the same pot with the meat juices, add the chopped onion and cabbage. Let them steam on low heat until wilted down and brown, about 20 minutes, stirring so they don't burn.

Add tomato paste, if using, and tomato sauce, if using, to the cabbage and onion mixture. Stir and cook until mixed together. Add broken-up canned tomatoes. Add one large can water and pour into pot. Add the meat back and cook slowly for 1 hour, stirring occasionally.

Add 4-6 tablespoons of brown sugar. Add sour salt (citric acid) or lemon juice, 1-2 tablespoons. Cook slowly for ½ hour longer.

Adjust sweet and sour flavor to personal taste with more sugar or sour salt (or lemon, if using).

Note: I put "optional" on the tomato paste and sauce because I no longer use them. It makes the soup too rich in tomato acid, and Jerry has a hard time digesting it. I use beef bouillon (salt-free) which gives it the richness and flavor it needs.

Note: When my mom lived on the East Coast, sour salt (citric acid) was easily available in the Kosher section of the grocery store, and she would keep me supplied. I found it in Texas at H-E-B Markets in the Hispanic section but never locally in the Hispanic sections; there are several brands of citric acid available online through Amazon. The soup is just as delicious made with fresh squeezed lemon juice. Just check to get the sweet and sour taste, and adjust accordingly.

Manischewitz Split Pea Soup

This is my easy way to make split pea soup.

This is the easy way to make split pea soup. Buy the Manischewitz mix in the Kosher section and follow the directions. The only thing I add is a couple of grated carrots and a bit of chopped onion. It takes a little watching and stirring, but in about an hour, delicious split pea soup. For a more filling meal, take a kielbasa rope, slice and brown for added flavor, and cook in the soup for the final 15 minutes.

Split Pea Soup

Broccoli and Zucchini Soup

This is a perfect way to get in your veggies.

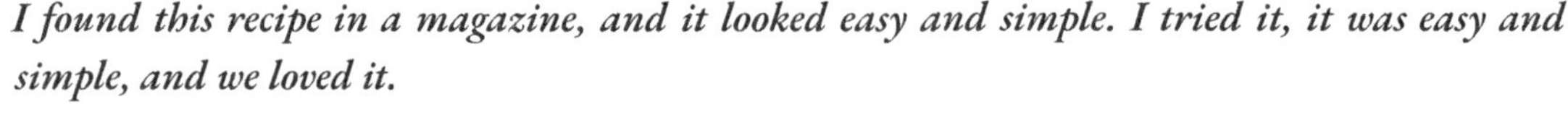

I found this recipe in a magazine, and it looked easy and simple. I tried it, it was easy and simple, and we loved it.

4 cups chicken broth
¾ pound broccoli florets
½ pound sliced zucchini
Salt and pepper to taste

In large stockpot, put in broth, broccoli, and zucchini and bring to a boil. Season to taste with salt and pepper, reduce heat to low, partially cover, and simmer for 15-20 minutes.

When cooked, purée vegetables in the pot, using an immersion blender.

To serve, ladle into bowls, drizzle with a little olive oil, and sprinkle with Parmesan cheese. It's amazingly delicious and so easy.

Canter's Style Bean and Barley Soup

*Canter's Deli is on Fairfax Avenue in Los Angeles,
which was the hub of Jewish life in L.A. in the 1950s and 1960s.*

When we were young adults, before children, and then when the children were little, we would take an occasional drive from San Bernardino to Los Angeles for a visit to Canter's Deli on Fairfax Avenue. The corned beef and pastrami sandwiches were awesome, and the chocolate chip rugelach was delicious, but the highlight of the trip was, without a doubt, a bowl of bean and barley soup.

A few years after our friends Susan and Bob moved back to Southern California, they sent me a recipe they thought I might like. I made that recipe once, and it was close, but I also made changes on my own. Here's my take on the soup.

8 cups chicken broth
2 carrots, peeled and diced
1 small onion, minced
2 celery ribs, diced
2 medium potatoes, peeled and diced
½ cup uncooked barley
¼ cup dried Lima beans
2 tablespoons butter
½ cup chicken meat, cut small
Salt, pepper, and garlic powder, to taste

Combine broth and vegetables in a large stockpot and bring to a boil. Add barley and Lima beans and bring back to low boil (simmer). Stir often to prevent sticking. Continue cooking 1 and ¾ hours, stirring occasionally.

Add the 2 tablespoons of butter, chicken, and seasonings. Cook another ½ hour or until barley and Lima beans are tender .

Serve and enjoy.

Manischewitz Vegetable Soup

This is a shortcut to making a delicious bean and barley soup.

A great and easy way to make and enjoy bean and barley soup is to buy a package of Manischewitz Vegetable Soup Mix that comes in a long, skinny package in the Kosher food aisle. It takes about two hours for the beans and barley to become thoroughly tender.

Follow the directions; however, because I like adding homemade touches, I sauté carrots, onions, potatoes, and celery in a bit of olive oil before I add the water, or again, for a richer soup, I'll sometimes add broth. There's a packet of seasonings and pasta that gets added the last 15 minutes of cooking time, and if you have any leftover cooked meat or chicken, cut it into bite sized pieces and throw it into the pot. It's a delicious and filling meal.

Salads

To most people, salads are healthy food.

Toss some raw vegetables in with some lettuce, add dressing, and serve. Add some leftover protein and you have a "diet" meal. Not so in Linda's kitchen. As Jerry's grandfather, his Zadie, used to say, "greens are for cows." This man, Harry Frank, ate red meat and potatoes only, smoked a cigar daily, drank his afternoon bourbon, and died at the age of 92. His daughter, Grandma Adele, said when he died, "I knew his eating habits were going to kill him." So much for salad greens.

Chicken, Egg, Salmon, or Tuna Salad

Jerry loves leftover chicken or salmon because he knows he'll get this salad for lunch the next day.

All kidding about salads aside, I make chicken or salmon or tuna salad very infrequently and only with canned tuna or leftover chicken or salmon. There is no recipe, but I'll tell you what I do.

Shred or chop finely the protein.

String and chop finely, 1-2 stalks celery.

Chop finely, small amount of onion.

Mix well and add 1-2 tablespoons of mayonnaise to taste. Salt and pepper to taste.

Optional additions:

Fruit: chopped apples, grapes, raisins
Nuts, such as walnuts or sliced almonds
Hard-boiled eggs, chopped

Serve with cherry tomatoes on bread or crackers. Now, that's a salad. Healthy? Maybe not so much, but very tasty and it's got protein, veggies, a little fat, and a few carbs, so it's a complete meal.

Note on optional additions: A lot of people like adding fruit to chicken salad, but when I make it for Jerry, I don't do anything but what I've written. As much as he loves eating fruit, he doesn't like fruit in salads. If you like fruit in chicken salad, by all means, add apples, grapes or raisins, and nuts, too, if you want some crunch. For a change of pace, hard boil a few eggs, cool them, and do the same thing.

Treeva's Salad (Super Salad)

As little girls growing up, Caren and Rachel loved eating and helping me make this salad.

When we were first married, we lived in a brand-new apartment building in San Bernardino at 17th or 18th and "G" Street. One neighbor in particular still stands out: she was Jewish, from Ohio, a bit older than us, and on a temporary work job. Her name was Treeva Krantz, and she shared a recipe with me that she made for a potluck. Kosher it isn't, but so yummy. My girls called this "Super Salad."

Incidentally, Treeva's claim to fame was that her cousin was in Hollywood, making movies. His name was Paul Newman. 'Nuff said: that's why I remember Treeva. Anyway, here's her salad recipe.

1 pound deli ham, thinly sliced

½ pound Swiss cheese, thinly sliced

2 chicken breasts, cooked and shredded

1 head Iceberg lettuce

1 head Romaine lettuce

One 8 ounce bottle Wishbone Italian dressing

One 8 ounce jar Miracle Whip (it looks like mayo but isn't), or, if using mayo, add 1 tablespoon sugar

Mix Wishbone dressing and Miracle Whip together until well blended and set aside. Wash lettuces and tear into bite-sized pieces. Cut ham and Swiss cheeses into thin strips.

Layer torn lettuces in a large shallow salad bowl. Top with ham, Swiss cheese, and shredded chicken. Pour dressing mixture over all and mix thoroughly.

Serve and enjoy!

Alice's Layered Salad

I've eaten many layered salads, but this combo of vegetables is my favorite.

When we first moved to our new home, our street was very social. A neighbor three houses away brought this layered salad to a potluck, and everyone loved it. This recipe is plenty for 16-20 people.

1 head Iceberg lettuce, torn
1 sweet onion, red or white, chopped
½ cup celery, chopped
½ cup bell pepper, any color, chopped (optional)
1 can water chestnuts, sliced, drained, and chopped
1 package frozen peas
2 cups mayonnaise
1 tablespoon sugar, mixed into mayo
½ cup Parmesan cheese
4 strips of crisp cooked bacon, crumbled

Using a large bowl, make two layers of all the veggies, ½ of each veggie per layer, then topping each layer with the lettuce. Cover the top layer with the mayonnaise and refrigerate overnight. ***Do Not Toss.***

Right before serving, top with the Parmesan cheese and bacon.

Serve by having guests use a large spoon to dig all the way down through the layers and scoop up a serving.

Linda's Potato Salad

I find most potato salads to be very heavy and hard to digest. Not this one.

I make a delicious Potato Salad that son-in-law Chris absolutely loves. I don't use eggs; however, they could certainly be added, but try it without: you'll like it.

Potatoes (see Note)
Onion
Celery
Mayonnaise (see Note)
Seasoned Rice Vinegar (see Note)
Salt, pepper, and garlic powder

Boil potatoes until done to your liking. We like soft and tender potatoes. Drain and cool, and then peel the potatoes.

While potatoes are cooking, slice and chop finely, sweet onion, whole if small, ½ if large.

String and chop finely, 2-3 celery stalks.

Cut the potatoes into chunks and layer half the potatoes in a large bowl. Add ½ of the veggies, season lightly, and mix. Add the second layer of potatoes, veggies, and season with salt, pepper, and garlic powder (lightly).

Sprinkle with seasoned rice vinegar and add small amount (one tablespoon is plenty) of mayonnaise and mix well. Taste and adjust seasoning. If too dry, sprinkle with a bit more vinegar.

Refrigerate and chill at least 4-6 hours or overnight. Taste for seasoning before serving.

Note: Buy large White or Yukon Gold potatoes, one for every 2 people, plus one extra for good measure. If the potatoes are small, buy one for each person plus two extra. Do not use russets.

Note: This is a dry potato salad. Don't use too much mayo or vinegar.

Linda's Potato Salad

Linda's Coleslaw

Coleslaw is quick, easy to make, and a healthy accompaniment to a picnic-style meal.

I have always liked a deli-type coleslaw, not one with heavy mayonnaise. After much experimenting, this is my take on a good coleslaw.

1 head cabbage (or two packages of ready-to-go sliced cabbage)
1-2 carrots, peeled and grated
A few slices onion, finely chopped
1 teaspoon sugar (or equivalent sugar substitute)
Seasoned rice vinegar (see Note)
1 tablespoon mayonnaise
Salt and pepper to taste (see Note)

Mix all ingredients well and sprinkle with sugar (or sugar substitute). Sprinkle with seasoned rice vinegar and mayonnaise.

Refrigerate a few hours or overnight. Mix well before serving.

Note: Some brands of rice vinegar contain corn syrup, which can cause negative reactions in people who are allergic to corn, so be sure to check ingredients.

Note: I find the vinegar has enough salt, but add more salt and pepper to taste.

Red Cabbage Coleslaw

I always get positive reactions from everyone who has tasted this.

My friend Marion got this special red coleslaw recipe from a friend whose parents had a summer hotel in Maine and were famous for this dish. The friend shared it with Marion, who shared it with me. I followed the recipe exactly (I don't have it anymore) and mixed and measured and cooked and cooled the dressing. And then I tasted it: Catalina dressing. And that's what I've used forevermore.

1 small red cabbage, chopped very thinly
¼ onion, sliced very thinly
1 bottle Catalina dressing

Mix cabbage and onion together. Add bottle of Catalina dressing. Refrigerate overnight to soften cabbage.

Serve and wait for the compliments.

Leonard's Chopped Salad

I have such fond memories of making this salad with my dad and brother.

My mom was the chief cook in our family, but my dad knew his way around the kitchen. He'd make breakfast on a weekend morning, or make a quick and easy lunch. This salad was one of his standbys, and my brother Jon and I loved it.

I used to make this for the girls and sometimes still make it for lunch. Brings back wonderful memories.

1 head of lettuce, thinly sliced and diced
Carrots, celery, onion, cucumber, and tomatoes, chopped
1 can of tuna, flaked into small pieces
Salt and pepper, to taste
Vinegar and oil, to taste

Add chopped veggies to the lettuce and mix well. Flake the tuna on top. Add salt, pepper, vinegar, and oil to taste. Toss and serve, and always so good.

When we go out to dinner, I love a wedge salad but I'm not a Bleu Cheese fan, so I ask for Ranch dressing. My very favorite restaurant salad is Ruth's Chris Chopped Salad. It has everything delicious in it, including hearts of palm and crispy onion strings. This salad is worth a visit, all by itself, to the restaurant. The steaks and sides are great, but this salad is extraordinary.

Homemade Salad Dressing

This is an easy salad dressing. I haven't bought bottled dressing in years.

Mom always served a salad with dinner that consisted of a wedge of Iceberg lettuce, sliced tomatoes, and cucumbers covered in bottled salad dressing. It's still one of my favorite salads although I make my own dressing.

½ cup olive oil
½ cup seasoned rice vinegar
2 tablespoons balsamic vinegar
Salt and pepper, to taste
Garlic powder, light dash
Italian seasoning (see Note), 2-3 shakes
½ teaspoon sugar
2 teaspoons Dijon mustard

Mix all ingredients and stir until emulsified. Taste for seasoning, and then pour over salad greens.

Bamma Freda's Lime Jell-O Salad

I haven't made this in years and to be truthful, there's not a Jell-O mold form in my kitchen. I'm including this since it was one of my mom's favorite recipes.

My mom (Bamma Freda) made a delicious Jell-O salad in the 1950s that she served with most holiday meals. Everyone loved it and always looked forward to her making it. She used a round Jell-O mold with round indentations on the bottom that she would fill with the cherries, so when it was unmolded, the purple cherries would be on top and looked beautiful against the light green Jell-O.

1 #2 can crushed pineapple, drained, with juice reserved
3 cups water
2 packages lime Jell-O
1 pint sour cream
1 can black, sweet, pitted cherries, drained

Combine 1 cup of reserved juice from crushed pineapple with water in a saucepan and bring to a boil. Pour in packages of Jell-O and stir till dissolved.

Place cherries in bottom of Jell-O mold. Carefully pour lime Jell-O mixture into mold. Chill until set. Serve.

Fruits

I've never met a fruit that I've truly loved.

I am not much of a fruit eater unless you count chocolate chips as a fruit: they're little and round and sort of look like berries. And chocolate is healthy, so they say. I actually do like some fruit, just not enough to buy any for myself. One or two bites of the preferred fruit, and I'm finished. Chocolate desserts served in restaurants with berries are a perfect example: a couple of bites of fruit and chocolate. Life is good.

Another example of a terrific fruit pairing is a Hawaiian drink called a Lava Flow: strawberry, pineapple, and coconut, and, lo and behold, there's three fruit servings in one day. Amazing how we can adjust our diet to maintain healthy eating. Just kidding; however Lava Flows are better than Mai Tai's or any other "tropical umbrella" drinks.

Lava Flow Drink in Hawaii

If someone cuts up fruit or if I cut up fruit for a platter, I'll eat cherries, strawberries, pineapple, green grapes, blackberries, watermelon, and apples, but only a few bites. They're colorful and make a beautiful presentation. I'll cut up cantaloupe, oranges, pears, kiwi, and peaches for other people, and that's about it. I like crunchy but nothing soft.

My absolute no-no, not ever, not even a bite: bananas. My theory is that it's an anti-banana gene that gets passed down through the generations. It's the taste, the texture, and the smell: and forget that it's high in potassium; potatoes have more potassium than bananas and they're more delicious.

Jerry, on the other hand, loves fruit. He eats fruit every day for breakfast, can't start his day without whatever fresh fruit is in season. He's especially happy in late July and August when his peach tree fruit is ripe for the picking. It's an amazing tree that's more like a one-tree orchard. One year he picked about 1,000 peaches from the tree.

Everyone we know and even people we don't know, gets peaches: neighbors, friends, family. Our local grocery store had a delightful young man who worked in the produce department. Jerry brought him a couple peaches to taste and the young man loved them. He would come over at the end of the season and strip the tree for us and take the peaches home to his wife and mother. We missed him when he transferred to another store.

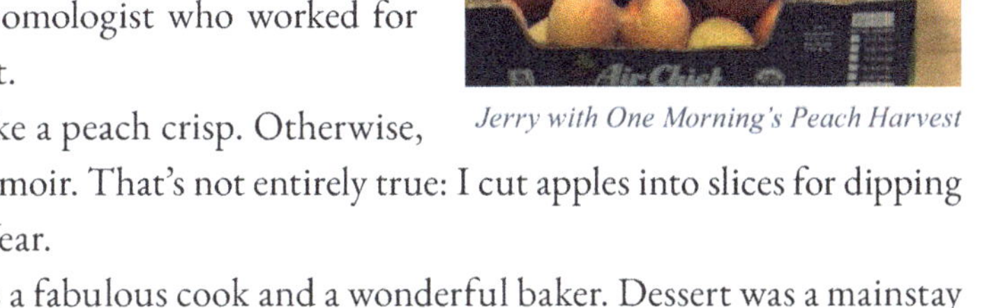
Jerry with One Morning's Peach Harvest

Lukas and Jah stripped the tree for us later, and Jah came over and picked the fruit throughout the harvest season. We didn't allow Jerry to climb the ladder anymore.

The tree was a giving tree; however, after 25 years in our backyard, it cracked, fell over, and died. We had to have it removed. No more peaches from the tree that was originally from Bob Fenton, friend, and a pomologist who worked for UC Davis Agriculture Department.

I'll eat the peaches when I make a peach crisp. Otherwise, there are no fruit recipes in this memoir. That's not entirely true: I cut apples into slices for dipping into honey for a good sweet New Year.

I need to say that my mom was a fabulous cook and a wonderful baker. Dessert was a mainstay in our house. She was a cake baker and occasionally made other desserts. Dinner always ended with something sweet. In her later years, she stopped baking and always served a Florida fruit salad which she bought in jars in the grocery store: refrigerated citrus sections in a very sweet heavy syrup.

Passover Charosets

This is always the preferred Passover fruit dish in our family.

During the Passover Seder, in the retelling of the story of Moses freeing the Children of Israel from the Pharaoh, we make a "sandwich" of matzo, horseradish, and an apple mixture, called Charosets, which represents the mortar used in the making of the bricks that the enslaved Israelis made. Charosets can be simple or complex: mine is a simple recipe although I don't really measure anything. I just kind of put it together, and it's easy and tasty.

Depending on how many people you're preparing for, here's what I do.

1-2 Fuji apples, peeled, cored, and shredded
¼-½ cup sweet kosher wine
¼-½ cup toasted walnuts (see Note), finely chopped
1-2 teaspoons honey
¼-½ teaspoon cinnamon
Pinch kosher salt

Combine all ingredients and refrigerate an hour or longer. Drain and serve.

Breakfast

My least favorite meal of the day, but here are some yummy options.

Jerry is helping me with this cookbook by giving me reminders of his favorite dishes. I really never thought of breakfast items because breakfast is not a big meal in our house. There are a couple of reasons for this: #1) I'm not a big breakfast eater, and #2) before Jerry and I got married, Grandma Adele told me that I had to get up early every morning and make Jerry his breakfast, which consisted of fruit, cereal in a bowl with milk, followed by a glass of milk. No, said I, he can do that himself.

Thus, when I made breakfast, it was a big deal. Now, not so much. If I'm cooking sausage or bacon, of course, I make enough for both of us. Jerry's usual breakfast is fruit and a couple of buttered Hawaiian buns. If I cook breakfast meats, he adds that to his normal breakfast. He doesn't drink milk anymore and he has never been a coffee drinker.

For me, breakfast is a cup of decaf coffee and whatever is left over in the refrigerator, i.e., pizza, Chinese food, chunk of pork chop or steak, or the aforementioned bacon or sausage.

Buttermilk Pancakes

These are delicious and were my introduction to thin pancakes.

Grandma Adele taught me how to make these but first, the story of these pancakes.

During World War II, there was a shortage of dairy products, and butter was rationed. To get more butter, Adele's mother, Jerry's Grandma Fern, would have her son, Uncle Bobby, invite fellow soldiers to their apartment in Chicago for buttermilk pancakes. Their entry fee: a stick of butter.

These pancakes are very thin: more like crepes. Grandma Adele had no recipe, so I watched, measured, and learned. This makes about 12 pancakes, enough for two people. I have tried doubling the recipe, but they're not as good, so I would make a batch and then a second one as needed.

---

1 egg, beaten
Pinch of salt
Pinch of baking soda
1 cup buttermilk
½ cup all-purpose flour

Handy Hint: I use a 4 cup measuring glass and I have a ¼ cup measuring scoop in the flour container, so I don't dirty anything else.

Mix beaten egg, salt, and baking soda in the large measuring cup. Add buttermilk and mix. Add flour and stir until combined.

Batter will be very loose. Make adjustments with flour or buttermilk after the first batch if too thick or too thin.

Heat a large skillet, and when hot, add 1 tablespoon of butter. When butter is sizzling, add batter in 3" circles, 3-4 pancakes at a time, depending on skillet size. Cook a couple of minutes until bubbles form, especially at the edges, and, after lifting slightly to check to make sure they're brown underneath, flip over and cook other side.

Do this until the batter is gone, adding more butter to the skillet each time. Turn down the heat after the first batch as pan will be very hot.

Serve with maple syrup or your choice of jelly.

Buttermilk Pancakes

Chocolate Chip Pancakes

No matter how early their day starts, every Saturday morning in daughter Leslie's household, her husband Bryce makes chocolate chip pancakes.

Speaking of pancakes, our son-in-law, Bryce, makes the world's best chocolate chip pancakes. I've tried to duplicate them, but he's got the technique down pat. I buy the same healthy Kodiak whole wheat pancake mix, follow the directions on the box, and add more chocolate chips just like he does, and they're nothing like his.

Finally, I mentioned it to him and he asked, "Do you use milk and eggs?" No, I don't, so no wonder his pancakes are better. Anyway, it's Bryce's recipe and technique, so I'll let you ask him. They are addicting, so be prepared for deliciousness. Just add lots and lots of chocolate chips.

Dutch Baby Pancakes

A delicious alternative to a traditional breakfast. Try it!

A high school friend of Rachel's taught me this recipe. Easy when feeding a large crowd as you can make two pans at once.

Leslie has a friend from her Coro Fellowship days, 1996-1997, who remembers me serving these to their group when they were up in northern California and some of them spent the night at our house. I don't remember how many of them there were, but I do remember bodies sprawled all over the house. The Dutch Babies are so good, they stay memorable.

---

3 tablespoons butter
3 eggs, beaten
¾ cup milk, room temperature
¾ cup all-purpose flour
1 tablespoon sugar
1 teaspoon vanilla extract
1 pinch salt
2 tablespoons confectioner's sugar (for serving)

Preheat oven to 400º F.

Place butter in 9x13" pan, and place in oven.

Combine eggs and milk in a bowl. Add flour, sugar, vanilla extract, and salt, and then whisk for 1 minute to remove lumps.

Carefully remove hot pan from oven, and swirl melted butter to coat. Pour batter into the hot pan and return to oven.

Bake in oven until pancake is puffed in the center and golden brown on edges, 20-25 minutes.

Dust with confectioner's sugar. Serve as is or topped with maple syrup or jelly.

Scrambled Eggs

Due to my food intolerance, I don't eat eggs anymore, but I've been told my scrambled eggs are quite tasty.

Everyone has their own way of making scrambled eggs so I'm not writing a recipe: just a few hints for making them delicious. I add a little water, not milk, when scrambling, and then, a little olive oil, maybe ¼ teaspoon for 2 eggs. It does something magical to the eggs. I just read about it recently and tried it. It makes the eggs soft and silky.

And, of course, cook in melted butter, low and slow, and stir with a wooden spoon. Salt and pepper to taste.

Grandchildren Micah, Hannah, and Elijah think my scrambled eggs are delicious.

Ham and Egg Omelette with Tomatoes

Breakfast Potatoes

Potatoes are probably one of my very favorite foods.
And they're loaded with potassium, so I don't have to eat bananas.

I usually make these when we're having breakfast for dinner, but sometimes I do make them for breakfast.

2 large Yukon Gold potatoes (see Note)
½ sweet white onion, diced
1 zucchini (optional), shredded
½ cup shredded cheese, your preference
¼ cup olive oil, preferably extra virgin olive oil
Salt, pepper, and garlic powder, to taste

Heat large skillet with olive oil. Add diced onions; lightly salt and pepper, and sprinkle with garlic powder. Add diced or shredded potatoes (and zucchini, if using), and season lightly.

Cook slowly, turning occasionally, letting everything brown but not burn, for about 20/25 minutes.

Sprinkle cheese on top, and serve.

Variation: For added protein, cook 2 eggs over-easy and serve on top of potatoes. Or make scrambled eggs to serve with the potatoes.

Note: For breakfast, I slice and dice the potatoes. For dinner, I grate the potatoes and zucchini. No reason, just preference. Either way works, and they're both delicious.

French Toast

I remember my mother making French Toast and serving it to me with grape jelly, which is still my favorite way to eat it.

Very rarely do we have challah in the house, but sometimes, when daughter, Leslie, is visiting from Texas, she makes challah. With leftovers, I make French Toast. Again, no recipe to follow but this is what I do.

1 egg, blended
1 teaspoon sugar
Cinnamon, 2 dashes
Challah, sliced

Mix egg, sugar, and cinnamon well. Soak challah slices in egg mixture until absorbed.

Melt butter in skillet, then add sliced challah. Turn when one side is browned, and cook other side.

Serve with maple syrup or jelly.

Matzo Brei

I grew up eating matzo brei; Jerry didn't. It took him years to decide he liked it after all.

During Passover, I make Matzo Brei (pronounced "Bry"), which is almost like making French Toast except it isn't. I make ours savory rather than sweet; however, I think it's how you grew up that determines how you like it.

1 matzo sheet per person
1-2 eggs per person
½ small onion, chopped (see Note)
1-2 tablespoons butter

Break up 1 matzo sheet per person. Soak in water and then wring water out.

Mix 1 or 2 eggs and soak matzo pieces in the eggs.

Sauté onion in skillet with butter until lightly browned, and then salt to taste.

Add matzo and egg mixture and stir well with onions. Turn and cook until matzo brei is cooked through and browned.

Serve with syrup and enjoy.

Note: If you like Matzo Brei sweet, don't use onion: just use cinnamon and sugar in egg-matzo mixture.

Lunch

Lunch is really an afterthought in our house. Leftovers when available or an occasional light frozen meal.

Lately, Jerry discovered he likes prepared California Rolls from the grocery store, so he picks up a package whenever we go. Otherwise, he eats lunchmeat ham, crackers, and cherry tomatoes for lunch. Leftover chicken or salmon get made into "salad" as described in the salad chapter, as do, very occasionally, canned tuna or hard-boiled eggs. Then this is what he eats with crackers and tomatoes.

One day in Texas, I made canned tomato soup and grilled cheese sandwiches for lunch for Micah, Hannah, and Elijah. They said they were "the very best grilled cheese sandwiches" they had ever had. So, I've added that to my title and I'm now "The best grilled cheese sandwich maker ever."

Here's my big secret recipe.

The Very Best Grilled Cheese Sandwiches

Grilled cheese sandwiches are loved by all my grandchildren.

2 slices of bread for each sandwich
2 slices American cheese for each sandwich
Butter

Take the bread and butter one side of each slice.

Put one slice, buttered side down, in a hot skillet.

Add 2 slices American cheese.

Top with other buttered slice, buttered side facing up.

Cook until golden brown on bottom. Flip over and cook other side until golden brown.

Put on plate and cut into triangles. Serve and wait for the compliments.

Vegetables

As I mentioned in the Fruit Section, I really do love my vegetables.

With the exception of a few actual recipes, I just roast or sauté most of the veggies we eat. I grew up eating only canned vegetables because that was what my mother served. Growing up in New York, in Brooklyn actually, canned vegetables were what was available to her as a child and young woman, and that was all she knew. Fresh vegetables were carrots, potatoes, celery, onions, and cabbage, which basically were used for making soup. She served canned corn, peas and carrots, green beans, spinach (yuk), and all were heated with their canned liquid in a pan.

Mom got introduced to fresh veggies after we moved to Boca Raton, Florida in the late 1940's. West of the small town that was Boca Raton at that time was a huge family-owned farm. My dad worked in the post office at the main postal counter, so he knew everyone who lived in Boca. Everyone in town came into the Post Office.

The farmers in the area would bring in huge boxes of fruits and vegetables for the postal workers, and Dad started bringing fresh vegetables home. Mom learned about cooking fresh vegetables, and cook them she did. To this day, I like my vegetables well cooked. I'm not a fan of crunchy cooked vegetables although I will eat raw cauliflower and peas from the pod. I can remember sitting with my mom and opening pea pods to remove the peas. I loved the raw peas and probably ate one for every one that went into the bowl.

Mom learned about cooking fresh corn on the cob; it took me many years to learn that cooking fresh corn on the cob takes just a few minutes.

One last thought: I always use fresh zucchini and Brussels sprouts and potatoes, but I love the Birds Eye C & W brand of frozen broccoli florets and Birds Eye C & W petite white corn.

Bamma Freda's Noodle Spinach Casserole

This is not a "heart-healthy" dish, but we sure enjoyed it whenever my mom made it.

My mom did make one very good vegetable casserole that I will include here, just so it's remembered.

8 ounces broad noodles
1 package frozen spinach
3 eggs, beaten
¾ stick butter or margarine, melted
1 cup unsweetened, nondairy coffee creamer (or low-fat Half-and-Half)
1 package Lipton Onion Soup (see Note)

Preheat oven to 350º F.

Cook noodles (not soft, about 4 minutes). Defrost spinach and squeeze out water. Mix together noodles, spinach, and onion soup mix.

Combine butter, eggs, and coffee creamer, and then pour over noodle spinach mixture. Mix well. Pour into 9x9" ungreased glass casserole dish. Bake at 350º F for 40-50 minutes until brown and bubbly.

Bammy's (that's me) Potato Latkes

One of my earliest memories is eating potato latkes (pancakes). My mom made these all the time.

Our group of friends held a Chanukah latke-making contest. There were four categories, and I won three of the four. I've been famous for my latkes ever since. What makes this so special is the joy I get from seeing the kids making latkes with me in the kitchen.

1 medium onion, peeled and grated

2 eggs, beaten

3 tablespoons potato pancake mix, such as Manischewitz or Streit's

3 tablespoons flour

Salt and pepper to taste

Garlic powder

Oil for frying

3-4 very large white or Yukon Gold potatoes plus one extra potato for good measure, grated (If potatoes are medium-sized, buy one per person plus a couple extra, see Note)

Add optional veggies for a different take on latkes (see Note)

1 zucchini (optional), grated

1 carrot (optional), grated

Grate potatoes, as well as zucchini and/or carrots (if using), and onion in a large bowl (see Note). Press lightly to drain some of the excess liquid. Add eggs and other ingredients. Mix well.

Heat ¼-½" oil in a large frying pan, replenishing oil as needed. Drop batter by spoonfuls into hot oil. Fry on each side until brown and crispy. Drain well on paper towels.

Serve with sour cream and/or applesauce (serves 6-8). Enjoy! Leftovers are always delicious the next day.

Note: I always use potatoes such as Yukon Gold or white potatoes. It's just my preference. The skins don't need to be peeled, and the flesh is smooth and not grainy.

Note: I had a small section of cabbage in the refrigerator and I chopped it into small pieces and added it to the latke batter. Nobody but me knew I did it and they were just as delicious as always with the added bonus of a few more veggies sneaking into the diet.

Note: I've always grated the potatoes and onions with a hand box grater, but a food processor also works. The past few years, grandson Lukas has come over and done the grating: such a mensch! And granddaughter Anya helps with the frying. Latkes always taste better with love.

Chanukah Potato Latkes

Potato Kugel

Jerry always preferred my latkes to kugel, but for kugel lovers, here's how to do it.

My mother, Bamma Freda, used to make potato kugel instead of latkes. It's the same latke batter but it gets baked in a round baking dish and cut into wedges, or baked in a 9x13" pan and cut into squares, depending on how many people are being served.

1 medium onion, peeled and grated

2 eggs, beaten

3 tablespoons potato pancake mix, such as Manischewitz or Streit's

3 tablespoons flour

Salt and pepper to taste

Garlic powder

Oil for frying

3-4 very large white or Yukon Gold potatoes plus one extra potato for good measure, grated (If potatoes are medium-sized, buy one per person plus a couple extra)

Add optional veggies for a different take on kugel (see Note)

1 zucchini (optional), grated

1 carrot (optional), grated

Preheat oven to 375º F.

Add 4 tablespoons of oil to bottom of the pan. Place it in the oven to heat the pan and oil. When the oil sizzles, remove the pan from the oven, and carefully pour kugel batter into pan. Pour another 2-3 tablespoons oil over batter and put into the hot oven for approximately 1 hour until set and cooked through.

Cut into wedges or squares and serve.

Vegetable Kugel

To turn this into a Vegetable Kugel, grate carrots and/or zucchini into the potato kugel batter, and mix well.

3-4 very large white or Yukon Gold potatoes plus one extra potato for good measure, grated (If potatoes are medium-sized, buy one per person plus a couple extra)

1 zucchini, grated

1 carrot, grated

1 medium onion, peeled and grated

2 eggs, beaten

3 tablespoons potato pancake mix, such as Manischewitz or Streit's

3 tablespoons flour

Salt and pepper to taste

Garlic powder

Oil for frying

Preheat oven to 375º F.

Add 4 tablespoons of oil to bottom of the pan. Place it in the oven to heat the pan and oil. When the oil sizzles, remove the pan from the oven, and carefully pour kugel batter into pan. Pour another 2-3 tablespoons oil over batter and put into the hot oven for approximately 1 hour until set and cooked through.

Cut into wedges or squares and serve.

Oven-Browned Potatoes

My mother, Bamma Freda, always served these, so I guess the "potato" doesn't fall far from the "tree."

For holiday or company meals, my go-to accompaniment has been oven-browned potatoes. So easy to do and everyone likes them. Now I buy the tiny little round white or gold potatoes in bags, but always in years past, I just cut up, depending on the size, into quarters or eighths, white or gold potatoes. Leave the skin on.

1 bag small white or gold potatoes, skin on, or larger potatoes cut into quarters or eighths

Olive oil

Salt and pepper

Garlic powder

Preheat oven to 350º F.

Place potatoes in a baking pan. Sprinkle with salt, pepper, and garlic powder. Sprinkle with olive oil.

Bake at 350º F for one hour, or at 400º F for 30-40 minutes until very browned, gently shaking pan occasionally to ensure even browning.

Very easy and delicious.

Roasted Vegetables

It was an amazing revelation when I discovered roasted vegetables.

Lately, I've taken to oven roasting vegetables: the sweetness and flavors are amazing. I pretty much do the same thing with cut up broccoli, zucchini rounds, Brussels sprouts, and potatoes cut into strips (oven fries.)

Preheat oven to 400º F.

Cover a sheet pan with parchment paper and spread out whatever veggies you're making. Don't crowd the pan as they need to roast, not steam. Season with salt, pepper, and garlic powder. Drizzle with olive oil. (see Note)

Bake at 400º F to caramelize until brown. Check at 30 minutes: flip veggies over and roast until done to taste. Serve with delicious add-ons if desired.

Delicious add-ons:

Broccoli: Lemon zest or lemon pepper seasoning
Zucchini: Parmesan cheese
Brussels sprouts: toasted pine nuts or almond slivers and/or bacon bits
Potato strips (oven fries) salt

Note: I put the cut-up pieces of vegetables into a veggie bag (from the produce department), and then add the seasonings and olive oil in the bag. I hold it closed and shake to cover the vegetable pieces. Then I dump everything onto the parchment paper-lined sheet pan and spread the veggies out. No muss, no fuss, no cleanup.

Orzo Pasta with Spinach and Tomatoes

When I learned that orzo was pasta and not rice, this became a favorite dish to serve.

When I was recovering from my knee replacement surgery and kidney failure in 2001-2002, I watched a lot of television. Food channels were becoming popular, and I recuperated watching TV cooking shows. Granddaughter Sarah was visiting when we saw this pasta dish, and it looked so good, we had to try it. It was good and so easy.

I always associate this with Sarah, so to me, it's Sarah's Orzo, and it's good served hot or cold.

---

1 substantial package of fresh baby spinach, with stems detached

1 container cherry tomatoes, halved

Zest from 1 or 2 lemons (use your judgment based on lemon size and desired lemon flavor)

2 cups of orzo pasta, boiled until al dente, drained

2 tablespoons of extra virgin olive oil

Juice from the zested lemon

½ English cucumber, peeled and cubed

1 red bell pepper (optional), cut into small slices

½ cup sweet white onion or ¼ cup red onion, finely chopped

A generous handful of fresh basil leaves, de-stemmed, sliced into fine strips

Salt and freshly ground pepper, to taste

Put the spinach leaves in a large mixing bowl. Arrange the tomatoes on top of the spinach. Sprinkle the lemon zest over the tomatoes.

Pour the hot, freshly drained orzo into the bowl, allowing the warmth of the pasta to gently wilt the spinach and warm the tomatoes while releasing the lemon zest's aroma.

Drizzle the olive oil and lemon juice over the orzo, tossing well to incorporate the vegetables and pasta evenly. Let cool to room temperature.

Before serving, fold in the basil leaves, cucumber, onion, and red bell pepper (if using), and season with salt and pepper to taste. Give it another toss, do a final taste test for seasoning adjustments, and serve your dish.

Marion's Vegetable Torte

Anything from my friend Marion's kitchen is always delicious.

This recipe is from my friend Marion. It is not a quick recipe, but it is easy, delicious, and it serves a crowd.

2 packages frozen spinach, cooked according to package instructions, drained and chopped

1-pound small zucchini, sliced

1 onion, chopped

8 ounces mushrooms, sliced

1-2 cloves garlic, crushed

¾ cup green olives, chopped

½ cup Parmesan cheese

½ bread crumbs, seasoned

4 eggs, slightly beaten

1 teaspoon Italian seasoning (see Note)

1 tablespoon olive oil

Preheat oven to 350º F.

Cook sliced zucchini, onions, mushrooms, and garlic in oil until soft.

In a large bowl, combine zucchini mixture, cooked drained spinach, and all remaining ingredients. Mix well. Turn mixture into a greased loaf pan and bake at 350º F for 45 minutes or until firm.

Cool, unmold, wrap in foil, and chill in refrigerator until completely cool. Cut into slices and serve.

Serves 8 with full slices or 16 with half slices. It's very rich and filling.

Corn on the Cob

Although I've tried the new method of cooking corn on the cob by placing the unshucked corn in the microwave for three or four minutes, I'm still a fan of cleaning it by hand and then cooking it in a pan of boiling water. This microwave method does work well for two ears of corn but becomes a chore when cooking large amounts of corn. However, the husks and silk do just slide right off so cleaning it is a breeze. And the corn is already cooked when taken out of the microwave. Serve, butter and salt and it's ready to go.

When cleaning by hand, place the cleaned ears of corn in a pot filled with cold water. Add a spoonful of sugar to the water — yes, sugar, never salt: salting the water when cooking results in tough corn — cover and bring to a rolling boil. Turn off heat and let sit for about ten minutes in the hot water. Remove, drain, and serve with butter and salt.

Sautéed Corn

This is my new favorite way to make corn.

One of Jerry's favorite vegetables is sautéed corn. Grandma Adele made it for him by opening a can of Niblets corn and cooking it in margarine until browned. And that's how I made it for him for years. Now, I've changed it up ever so slightly. Again, very quick and easy. Jerry thinks it's "gourmet," and I know how quick and easy it is to make, and it makes him happy.

½ frozen bag of Birds Eye C & W (or other brand) frozen sweet white corn
¼ onion, chopped
1 tablespoon butter
Salt and pepper
Garlic powder

Heat butter in a skillet on medium heat. Add the onion and sauté a few minutes. Add corn and seasonings. Stir until corn and onions are brown.

Sautéed Cabbage

I love cabbage. I make it in soup, stuffed cabbage, and now sautéed.

This is the easiest dish to make and so good, served by itself or with any of the delicious additions.

2 tablespoons butter
½ head green cabbage, sliced and chopped
½ onion, chopped
Salt, pepper, and garlic powder
Broad egg noodles (optional), cooked and drained

Melt butter in a stockpot. Add onion, cabbage, and seasonings. Cook on medium low heat, stirring occasionally, 15-20 minutes.

Serve as is, or mix in cooked, drained noodles and sauté until the noodles get brown.

Suggested additions: Cooked bacon, kielbasa sausage, or any leftover meat turn this into a one-pot, complete meal, especially with the noodles.

Asparagus

I'm always so excited to see the first spring asparagus crop in the grocery stores.

Asparagus is an amazing vegetable that people either love or hate. I grew up as a hater because the only asparagus I had growing up was white asparagus from a can. To my tastebuds as a child, this was not pleasant. Then I tried it in a restaurant, served bright green and tender, with, I'm sure, some sort of sauce on it. It's now a springtime treat when the first asparagus of the season arrives in the grocery store. And it's so simple to make.

Granddaughter Anya served, as an appetizer, pickled asparagus from a jar. It was delicious. I found it in the grocery store where the olives and pickles are displayed.

I prefer the medium-sized stalks, while others like the thin baby-sized stalks. Personal preference is the key here.

1 bunch asparagus
Salt and pepper
Balsamic vinegar
Olive oil

Hold each stalk and bend it to let it break off where it's tender.

Heat the oil in a skillet and lay in the asparagus. Season with salt and pepper. Let lightly cook for a few minutes and, using a spatula, turn the stalks over. Pour a scant ¼ cup water in and steam as water dissolves. The asparagus should be bright green and tender.

Remove from heat and drizzle with balsamic vinegar.

Spinach Soufflé

Easy to heat and serve, and makes an elegant accompaniment to fish, lamb, beef, pork, or chicken (the last of which I don't eat).

Another great vegetable to serve is frozen Stouffer's Spinach Soufflé. It's microwaved and takes just a few minutes and is so good. A quick and easy shortcut to a delicious vegetable. It's usually found in the frozen food aisle where Stouffer's dinners are, not where the frozen vegetables are displayed.

Fried Green Tomatoes

Make sure, as the cook, to eat a few yourself as you're making them, or you might not get any. They are delicious and a special treat.

Most people know about Fried Green Tomatoes from the movie or the book Fried Green Tomatoes at the Whistle Stop Café, by Fannie Flagg. I learned about fried green tomatoes when we lived in Pompano Beach, Florida in 1962-1964. It is definitely a southern region recipe, introduced to me by our across-the-courtyard neighbors who came from Alabama.

Daughter Rachel asked me to include these because she remembers eating and liking them. Hmmm! Maybe it's because I learned how to make them when I was pregnant with her?

Daughter Leslie learned to love these at The Monster Barbecue in Syracuse, NY, when she was there attending school. We went twice on our trip to attend her graduation. (This was when we met Bryce for the first time and learned what a chocolate lover he was. Ask him about Friendly's Ice Cream parlor.)

The hardest part of making fried green tomatoes is finding the green tomatoes. Most grocery stores do not have them; however, if you grow tomatoes or know someone who does, just pick them early before they turn red.

There are lots of recipes online but I think those recipes take a simple dish and turn it into something very complicated.

Most recipes call for cornmeal, milk, eggs, breadcrumbs, flour, seasonings, oil for frying and of course, the green tomatoes. My pantry never has cornmeal and we never have milk of any kind in the refrigerator, yet I can make delicious fried green tomatoes.

The technique involves creating a coating that sticks to the tomatoes before frying them. I make a coating yet keep it simple, but it is a process.

4-5 nice sized green tomatoes, sliced into ¼" – ⅓" pieces, for a total of 16-20 pieces
½ cup all-purpose flour
Salt, pepper, garlic powder
Any additional spices to taste
2 eggs, beaten
Milk (optional)
Panko (or other) unseasoned breadcrumbs

Put the flour into a vegetable bag and season with salt, pepper, garlic powder, and any other seasoning you like, especially if you like a little spice. Put the sliced tomatoes into the bag and gently shake until all are covered in the seasoned flour mixture. Remove the tomato slices and place on waxed paper.

Put the beaten eggs in a shallow dish. Add a little milk (if using). Mix well.

Put the Panko (or other) breadcrumbs into a second shallow dish. Season.

Using one hand as your "wet" dipping hand, take the floured tomato slices and dip them into the eggs and then into the breadcrumbs until the tomato slices are covered completely. Place on wire racks to dry until ready to fry.

Most people deep-fry these but I don't like using much oil, so I use a shallow skillet. Heat enough oil to come up at least halfway up the slices and cook them until the bottom side is brown. Do not crowd the pan. Turn, finish cooking, and drain on paper towels. Keep warm while you fry the next batch.

Serve with a dipping sauce of your choice, e.g., Ranch or Thousand Island dressing, or a chipotle sauce.

Carrot Casserole

This is Alice's carrot casserole recipe as given to me.
Don't count the calories: it's an occasional dish, not an everyday thing.

At a dinner gathering one evening, many years ago, a lovely lady named Alice served this carrot dish. It tasted heavenly, and she shared her recipe. I know that generally no one thinks of carrots as "heavenly," but try this and you'll be convinced.

Alice and her husband, Hans, were German Jews who managed to leave Germany and find refuge in Shanghai, China during World War II. Although they survived and life was not easy in Shanghai, Alice was a sweet, kind woman who always cared about others. Her daughter was my friend Myrna, who is mentioned in the Mexican Cookie recipe.

12 large carrots, cut into large pieces
1 small onion, diced
1 tablespoon butter
½ cup butter, softened
1 egg, beaten
Salt and pepper to taste
1 clove garlic, minced
2 cups Ritz crackers, crushed
1 cup cheddar cheese, shredded

Preheat oven to 325º F.

Cook carrots in boiling water until soft. Drain well and mash.

Sauté onions over medium-high heat in the tablespoon of butter until very soft.

In a large bowl, combine carrots, onions, softened butter, egg, salt, pepper, and garlic. Mix well.

Spray an 8x8" Pyrex dish with nonstick spray. Place carrot mixture in dish and top with crackers and cheese. Bake at 325º F for 25-30 minutes.

Cut into nine portions, although it serves eight with just a little bit left over for whoever wants just a little bit more. Yes, it's that good.

Red Pepper and Onion Relish

I first tasted this when we bought a jar while on vacation in Hawaii.

This is a condiment that I buy online that is so delicious when served with grilled steak or lamb chops. It's sweet and just a little bit zingy and adds so much flavor. I'm sure there are many companies that make something like this; however, I really like the Robert Rothschild Farms product. I order it online directly from the company (or you can get it from Amazon).

There was a steakhouse that we used to enjoy that served their own relish with their steaks, so I went all in trying to duplicate it with no success. Then I tried a jar of this red pepper and onion relish, and it was perfect, and I've been hooked ever since. As Mikey on the older commercials would say, "Try it: you'll like it."

Speaking of vegetables, Jerry reminded me of the story about vegetables that has become part of our family's history. Our eldest daughter Caren was a very early and vocal talker. She knew her words for all foods: apples were apples, pears were pears, corn was corn, beans were beans; you get the picture, however peas, the easiest word of all, were not peas. They were "yebedals." Peas are still known as "yebedals" in our home.

Meats, Seafood, and Mains

Proteins are my favorite foods (except vegetables: those are yummy, too).

Jerry and I are both carnivores: we would eat beef every day if we could, but we are mindful about our diets, and steak is now a once a week treat. Roasts are for company or holiday meals, and meatloaf (sorry, Rachel: she doesn't like it) is comfort food.

Since I no longer eat chicken, it's always a treat for Jerry when someone is going to Costco and offers to shop for us. He eats chicken for a few meals, and I freeze the legs and thighs for when I make chicken soup. One piece gives the soup great flavor. After 2-3 days of chicken, I chop the leftovers and make chicken salad.

Pork has become our "other white meat," and I have finally learned how to buy and cook it so that's it's delicious. Salmon is just about the only fish I cook, and it's only the Salmon Milano from Costco. Always comes out delicious and not fishy because it's already been skinned.

Shrimp is my new "go to" for a quick and easy meal, especially if I've neglected to defrost anything else.

We do eat a variety of proteins served with our vegetables for a balanced diet. We eat well and as we've discovered during these years of Covid, our freezers are full. Rice or potatoes round out our meals as we're not afraid of a few carbs.

Stir Fry

I love making stir-fries. It's an easy way to combine meats and vegetables and have a nutritious meal.

Most of my dinners that I prepare now do not require recipes but rather are techniques. A stir fry is a stir fry whether it's with beef, pork, chicken, or shrimp.

Cut all vegetables that you're using into bite-sized pieces and have them ready. Cut protein of choice into bite-sized pieces and season.

Heat oil until very hot in a skillet or wok, and add protein and stir until almost cooked. Remove from pan and set aside.

Heat more oil and stir fry veggies, starting with ones that require more time, then add all other veggies.

Add protein back into pan and mix.

Add whatever sauce you're using, taste for seasonings and serve over rice or your choice of accompaniment.

Beef and Broccoli Stir Fry

Shrimp and Broccoli Stir Fry

Shrimp

I love buying the larger 16-20 pieces, two-pound bags of frozen shrimp from our local grocery store.

I cook shrimp using either Italian seasonings or as scampi in a wine, butter, and capers sauce. I also use Asian seasonings and sauces with shrimp. Throw in some veggies, serve over rice, and it's another quick dinner.

Again, these are techniques, rather than recipes. I get food suggestions and recipes from AllRecipes, and if it looks interesting, I'll try it. If it calls for chicken, I use shrimp and adjust cooking times accordingly.

One day the website sent their versions of restaurant meals and one was called "Firecracker Chicken," a hot and fried spicy chicken. I read it and thought if I left out the spicy peppers, made it with shrimp and skillet-cooked instead of deep frying, it might be good. The new technique was to dredge the shrimp in seasoned corn starch before cooking. The shrimp turned out crispy and crunchy, and we liked it.

Italian-Seasoned Shrimp and Rice Pilaf

Shrimp Enchiladas

This is my way of cooking: taking a technique and adapting it to other dishes.

While walking the frozen food section, I saw a package of frozen chicken enchiladas in green sauce and thought, I bet I can make this using shrimp. I used to love green chicken enchiladas. So, no recipe but here's what I did, and it turned out delicious.

I bought a can of mild green enchilada sauce and followed the instructions for cooking times and proportions of food. Shredded chicken became sautéed shrimp, cut into bite-sized pieces, with sautéed chopped onion. Instead of rolling the shrimp/onion mixture in flour tortillas, I had small, street taco sized corn tortillas, so I used those. They were too small to roll so I cut them in half and made layers, in a square baking dish, of tortillas, shrimp, and shredded cheese, and layered them like a lasagna. I covered it all with the canned green enchilada sauce and cheese, and baked the dish per the directions on the can. It was delicious and a new favorite dinner was born.

The second time I made it, I threw some frozen corn into the shrimp/onion mixture. It made it even better.

That's how I cook... and that's how we eat.

Crab Cakes

Homemade crab cakes are so delicious: time-consuming, maybe, but worth the work.

I read an AARP article dated March/April 2009. It told the story of the meeting of author Pat Conroy and author Cassandra King. She writes, "Pat said his crab cakes were so good I would want to marry him after tasting them. They were, and I did." I thought what a cute story that was.

Jerry always loved crab cakes, but they're almost always made in restaurants with bell peppers, and he can't digest the acids in bell peppers. So I started working on a way to make them tasty but suitable for our dietary needs. Here's what I came up with.

1 pound lump crabmeat (from the plastic tub at Costco). (Don't use canned crab meat as it is too chopped and watery.)

¼ cup sweet white onion, finely chopped

1 lemon, divided

Salt and pepper

1 large egg white

Flour

5 tablespoons butter

2 tablespoons capers

Put crabmeat in a bowl; pick over for shells. Add onion and mix well. Squeeze 1 wedge of lemon over crab and onion; salt and pepper lightly.

In a small dish, beat egg white until foamy. Pour over crab and mix in. Using as little flour as possible, 2 tablespoons give or take, add to crab and gently mix together. Form mixture into four crab cakes, or smaller if serving as appetizers. Refrigerate for one hour.

Melt 2-3 tablespoons of butter in a flat, heavy skillet, until sizzling and just beginning to brown. Carefully add crab cakes. Brown on one side until crispy; turn carefully and brown the other side, then remove to a platter.

To make a sauce, add remaining 2 tablespoons butter to the hot skillet, stirring to dislodge any crab bits still stuck to the skillet. When butter begins to brown, squeeze in juice of ½ lemon and turn off the heat. Throw in capers and toss. Pour this very small amount of sauce over the crab cakes.

This makes four very large crab cakes, over 4 ounces each or as an appetizer, 8 two-ounce or 16 one-ounce crab cakes.

I like serving these on a bed of lettuce that's been lightly seasoned with olive oil and seasoned with Asian vinegar, but they're delicious just on a plate as an entrée with rice pilaf and a green vegetable. These really are delicious. However, they are very rich, so we discovered one crab cake per person was enough for us. The other two get reheated for lunch the next day.

Jerry wants me to add that restaurant crab cakes are never very good: he likes mine much better.

Chicken

I'm including a couple of chicken dishes that used to be family favorites. I don't make them any longer (food intolerance), but they were sure good.

Mildred's Chicken

Stewed chicken may not be on your typical restaurant menu, but it's a wonderful down-home Southern dish.

My friend Marion had a housekeeper/babysitter in the late 1960's when her son was a little boy. Her name was Mildred, and she was from Mississippi. She made this chicken, and we all loved it. I remembered some of how to do it so I called Marion and asked her what she remembered, and together we came up with this. Then, just for fun, I googled Southern Stewed Chicken and, with only slight variations in the seasonings, up came Mildred's Chicken. Amazing what's on the Internet.

The only difference was she used a can of cream of chicken or cream of mushroom soup, (it was the 1960's after all) and the Internet recipe just used extra chicken broth and more flour to thicken the sauce.

1 whole chicken, cut into parts, or use all white or dark meat, depending on your family's preference

Salt and pepper

Garlic powder

Onion powder

Poultry seasoning (see Note),

Italian seasoning (see Note)

¼ cup vegetable oil

½ stick butter

1 onion, chopped

2 celery stalks, chopped

¼ cup flour

1 can chicken broth

1 can condensed cream of chicken soup or cream of mushroom soup (see Note)

1 can water

Season chicken heavily with all the seasonings: this will flavor the pot of food.

Heat oil in large deep stockpot and darkly brown chicken, skin down to start and then turn over, for 3-4 minutes. Remove chicken to plate.

Add butter to hot pan, let it melt, and then add onion & celery and sauté 2-3 minutes.

Sprinkle in flour and stir 2 minutes. Stir in broth, condensed soup, and water, and mix well.

Add chicken back into pot, making sure the sauce covers it all. Bring to low boil (simmer). Cover and cook 1 hour, stirring occasionally. Taste for seasoning, and adjust if necessary.

Serve over rice or noodles.

Sticky Chicken

Granddaughter Sarah is now an adult, but "sticky chicken" is still one of her favorites.

Another easy chicken recipe from the 1980s was what Granddaughter Sarah called "sticky chicken" because it was finger food that stuck to your hands. Here's my version of the dish.

2 packages chicken wings, separated and tips removed, or 1 whole cut up chicken, or parts

1 8-ounce jar apricot preserves

1 8-ounce bottle Catalina dressing

1 package Lipton Onion soup dry mix (see Note)

Preheat oven to 350º F

Combine preserves, dressing, and onion soup mix together in large bowl. Add chicken and stir well so all parts are covered.

Place chicken on two parchment-covered sheet pans. (The parchment paper is so the sugar doesn't ruin the pans. This I learned the hard way after ruining many pans.) Bake at 350º F for 1 hour.

Serve and enjoy. Easy company dinner or, as wings, for appetizers.

Beef

I grew up eating a lot of chicken, but my mom's beef meals were always my favorites.

When serving a large crowd or for a holiday meal, brisket is the way to go. A little prep work, and into the oven it goes for minimum of two hours. A little more work, and it's ready for serving the next day. It always tastes better the next day so plan accordingly.

Brisket

This was always an inexpensive cut of beef, but not anymore.
Texas Bar-B-Que has made it scarce.

A friend recently reminded me of the time, about 40 years ago, that I invited her over for dinner when her husband was working out of town. She accepted and was very chagrined to discover that I was making brisket. She remembered that her mother's brisket was always tough and tasteless, and so she tried to wiggle out of the invitation. Jerry convinced her to come since she had never tasted Linda's (my) brisket. She came, she loved it, and has been telling this story ever since.

Brisket is a tough cut of meat and must be cooked slowly, covered in a roasting pan with plenty of liquid. This technique is called braising.

I still use my large blue speckled, covered, enamel roasting pan that I got when we got married when I make a brisket. I always thought these roasting pans came in one size only: huge. I didn't realize they came in smaller sizes until Grandma Adele started using a tiny blue speckled roasting pan since she was cooking for herself only. I now have it and use it when I'm making a pot roast. It's the cutest little pan and I still get a hoot out of using it.

1 large whole brisket 5-6 pounds
1 package Lipton onion soup mix (see Note)
1 can tomato sauce
1 large onion, diced
Salt, pepper, and garlic powder

Preheat oven to 350º F.

Put the onion on the bottom of a roasting pan, reserving ½ cup. Place the brisket on the onions and season. Sprinkle the onion soup mix over the meat . Top with reserved onions. Pour tomato sauce and 2 sauce cans of water over brisket. Cover and cook in oven at 350º F for 1 ½ -2 hours.

Remove from oven and cool. Slice and put back into roasting pan. Refrigerate overnight.

The following day, remove as much fat as possible. Bring to room temperature 2 hours before additional cooking. Cook 1 more hour at 350º F.

Serve.

One year for a Passover potluck, we were asked to bring a dish specifically for Passover along with the recipe. So I added ½ jar of horseradish to the top of the meat before adding the onion soup mix and tomato sauce and water. It turned out delicious but not spicy.

I wrote out my brisket recipe calling it, "Why is this brisket different from all other brisket?" and it was a hit with everyone. All I did was add the horseradish.

Two brisket versions for the price of one.

Roasting Pans

Standing Rib Roast

This is a family favorite, but because of the high-fat content, it's become a once-a-year treat. Oh, so yummy!

I always overcooked my roasts but this technique — starting it cooking, turning off the oven, letting it cook by residual heat, and then turning on the heat for final cooking and browning — really works. The inside is pink and the outer slices are cooked through. If you like rare meat, cut the first and last oven times by 2 minutes per pound for each roasting.

I send thanks to a friend's son for teaching me his technique for making a standing rib roast. Thank you, Eric Raffin.

1 five pound standing rib roast
Salt, pepper, and garlic powder

Remove roast from refrigerator and allow to stand at room temperature for at least 1 hour.

Preheat oven to 375º F.

Rub roast very heavily with the seasonings. Place it in a roasting pan with rib side down. Roast for 1 hour or 12 minutes per pound if larger than 5 pounds (10 minutes per pound for rare meat).

And end of cooking time, turn off oven, but leave roast in oven. DO NOT open oven door but leave roast in oven for a minimum of 3 hours. (see Note)

When getting ready to serve, without opening oven door, turn oven temperature to 375º F again, and roast another 20-30 minutes or 4-6 minutes per pound if roast is larger than 5 pounds, counting the preheating time.

Let stand 20 minutes before slicing.

Unless you have a second oven, have others bring the side dishes. Follow the instructions, and this is foolproof, tender, and delicious every time.

Note: IMPORTANT: DO NOT remove roast or open oven door from the time roast is put in oven until ready to serve. This is about a 5-hour process, not counting the room temperature standing time.

Prime Rib with Latkes and Carrots

Tri-Tip Roast

I learned about this cut of meat 50 years ago while living in San Bernardino.
It was a "new" cut of beef that became all the rage.

Tri-tip roast got its start in the Santa Maria, California area at ranches and restaurants along the coast. The meat is heavily seasoned with more spices than I use as a rub. Then cooked and served with tortillas, fresh salsa, beans, and rice.

It's a fun and easy way to feed a crowd. And it's much quicker and easier than brisket or standing rib roast.

1 tri-tip roast, about 2-2 ½ pounds
Season meat with salt, pepper, and garlic powder

Preheat oven to 400º F.

Roast for 20 minutes per pound, uncovered. Remove from oven, leave in pan, and let rest for 20 minutes before slicing.

Serves 4-6 people.

You can make two in same pan with the same timing for larger groups. I like it thinly sliced. This can also be done on the barbecue grill with the same timing.

Pot Roast or Beef Stew

Cooking a pot roast or beef stew may be simple food, but it sure makes the house smell good.

In contrast to tender cuts of beef, pot roast or beef stew uses a tough cut of beef which is cooked low and slow in liquid for hours (braising). I buy a beef chuck roast, about 2-2 ½ pounds and either chunk it myself into pieces for beef stew or leave it whole for pot roast.

Beef chuck roast, 2-2 ½ pounds
1 onion, chopped
1 pound carrots, peeled and cut in large pieces
4-5 medium potatoes, cut into quarters
1 package beef stew seasoning mix (see Note)

For Pot Roast:

Preheat oven to 325º F.

Brown the meat, seasoning with salt, pepper, and garlic powder. Put onion over meat. Add package of beef stew seasoning mix and 1 ½ cups of water. Cover and cook in oven for 1 ½ hours at 325º F.

Add carrots and potatoes to roasting pan, cover, and cook another hour.

For Beef Stew:

Brown the meat, seasoning with salt, pepper, and garlic powder. Put onion over meat. Leave browned meat in stockpot. Sprinkle 1 package beef stew seasoning (see Note) over meat and add 2 cups water. Cook on stovetop, low and slow (simmer) for 1 hour, stirring occasionally. Add carrots and potatoes, and cook another hour slowly.

Delicious meal either way with very tender meat.

I made a pot roast for dinner last night (with enough for dinner tonight) because it was cold and raining. I seasoned the meat with a little salt and garlic powder and browned it in a skillet with a little olive oil. Then I browned some diced onion, seasoned it with a little more garlic powder and salt, in a bit more olive oil, in the same pan. Everything went into the small roasting pan, along with a packet of Lipton onion soup mix and a cup of water mixed with a squeeze of ketchup. I roasted it covered, low and slow, 325º F for 1-½ hours. Oh, my, the house smelled so good.

While it was roasting, I peeled and cut up carrots and potatoes and tossed them in the roasting pan for another hour. The vegetables were done perfectly, and the meat was oh so tender. Jerry was heading into the kitchen at about 5:30 pm so I asked him to shut off the oven. Fifteen minutes later, he declared he was hungry and wanted to eat: this is the man who likes to eat around 7:00 p.m. Real cooking gets to him every time although I must admit, the house did smell very good. And dinner was delicious.

Meatloaf

This is my ultimate comfort food. I don't know why: it just is.

Meatloaf is a comfort food for me, and I enjoy making it for us and others also. It's my go-to meal when someone's been sick or had surgery and I'm bringing them dinner. (Sorry, Rachel. I didn't cook for you when you had surgery, but I knew better than to bring you a meatloaf. Besides, you have a fabulous cook in your own house. Shout out to Jah, who shares his wonderful cooking skills with us and always sharpens my knives for me.)

With a few personal changes that I've made to accommodate our taste buds, this is the basic meatloaf recipe that my mother always made. Mom also grated a potato and a carrot into her meatloaf, along with a grated raw onion. Even though they cooked in the meatloaf, the raw veggies did not agree with Jerry so I started sautéing them first. He prefers just the cooked onions, but sometimes I do grate a small potato and/or a carrot in with the onions and sauté them all together.

Jerry's mom, Grandma Adele, had a definitely different approach to her meatloaf. She added 3-4 hard boiled eggs to her meatloaf, which was disgusting to me, but I've never been an egg lover. She'd put half of her ground beef into a loaf pan, pat it down, lay the hard-boiled eggs end to end and then cover them with the remaining meat. It was always hard and dry, but it did have a slice of egg in every slice of meatloaf. It looked pretty but was just not for me.

I usually buy ground beef or turkey. I use Italian seasoning, ketchup instead of tomato paste (which my mom used in everything), and salt-free beef bouillon powder dissolved in a little water in place of the stock. I also add a little brown sugar to the ketchup on top. Gives it a nice flavor.

As I said earlier, this is cooking, not baking. As long as the basic proportions are consistent, the food will be delicious. This recipe gives us each 2 dinners and usually a small portion left over for both of us to have lunch.

---

1 tablespoon olive oil

2 cups onions (2 onions), chopped

½ teaspoon Italian seasoning (see Note)

½ teaspoon garlic powder

2 teaspoons kosher salt

1 teaspoon ground pepper

3 tablespoons Worcestershire sauce (see Note)

⅓ cup canned stock or broth (or as I said above, salt-free bouillon powder)

1 big squirt of ketchup

1 ½ pounds ground chuck (85% lean) or 1 ½ pounds ground turkey (see Note)

½ cup plain dry breadcrumbs (I like Panko)

2 large eggs, beaten

½ cup ketchup

Brown sugar (optional), and only a small amount, for taste

Preheat oven to 325º F.

Heat the olive oil in skillet and add the onions (and other veggies if you're using them) and the Italian seasoning, garlic powder, and salt and pepper. Cook over low heat, stirring occasionally, for 8-10 minutes, until onions are translucent but not brown.

Off the heat, add the Worcestershire sauce, chicken stock, and tomato paste. Combine and allow to cool.

In large bowl, combine the ground beef (or turkey), cooled onion and/or vegetable mixture, bread crumbs, and eggs; and mix lightly with a fork. Don't mash the ingredients or the meatloaf will be dense.

Cover a sheet pan with parchment paper and turn meat into pan. Don't use a loaf pan. Shape into a rectangular, thin loaf. Spread ketchup, with or without the brown sugar, evenly on top and bake for 1 hour at 325º F or until internal temperature is 160º F and the meat is cooked through.

Serve and enjoy.

Note: I prefer 85/15 ground beef but occasionally buy ground turkey.

Stuffed Cabbage Rolls

*I associate cabbage rolls with Jewish Eastern-European cooking.
My mom loved making cabbage rolls.*

I used to make these a few times a year until I discovered that I was the only one in the family who enjoyed them, and they're very labor intensive. Cabbage soup satisfies my taste buds with the sweet and sour sauce that the cabbage rolls are cooked in. Very similar in taste. I'm thinking that meatballs thrown into the cabbage soup for the last 20-30 minutes of cooking might be a very easy alternative to actual cabbage rolls.

I took a cooking class from our Congregation's "Kitchen Maven," and she taught us the easiest way to take the head of cabbage apart for the folding and rolling of stuffed cabbage. Instead of struggling to cut the core out of the raw cabbage and then place it in boiling water to soften the leaves: Do this... Place the cabbage head upside down in a large deep bowl with a couple inches of water and place it the microwave on high for 10 minutes. Take it out, let it cool, cut out the core easily, and peel off the leaves. It's an amazing technique and it works.

Otherwise, if you want to make stuffed cabbage, the Internet will give you all the recipes you will ever want.

Stuffed Cabbage Rolls

Street Tacos

We eat tacos any day of the week, not just on Taco Tuesday.

We find the street taco-sized tortillas are the perfect size for us. If I buy corn tortillas, I call them "tacos," flour tortillas, and I'm making "fajitas," but I do the same thing regardless. This is adapted for the two of us, so double or triple the amounts depending on your family's servings needed and their appetites. Sometimes I brown the corn tortillas in a little oil, and other times we eat them soft. Whatever your preference is what you do.

½ pound ground beef
1 small potato, shredded (see Note)
¼ medium onion, diced
¼ packet taco seasoning (see Note)
Shredded Mexican blend cheese (see Note)
Diced tomatoes
Guacamole
Salt, pepper, and garlic powder

Season and brown the beef, potato, and onion in a skillet on medium-high heat until the meat is cooked and the veggies are soft. Add taco seasoning and small amount of water, and stir until water is gone.

Sprinkle cheese over tortillas and microwave 30 seconds until cheese is melted. Spoon meat mixture on cheese-topped tortillas.

Top with guacamole and tomatoes. Serve by folding or rolling up tortillas.

This is a very quick and easy dinner. It may not be authentic but it is very tasty.

Note: At this point, you're probably wondering about the potato...it's a trick that was taught to me many years ago by a lovely young woman who provided childcare for us. It smooths out the meat, adds body to the meat mixture, and stretches out the servings to feed more people. It was a trick she learned from her family, and I've adopted it and have used it ever since.

Street Tacos

Other Meats

Scallopini

If you're ever mad at anyone, make scallopini. All that pounding will relieve any anger.

This recipe, with changes made over time to accommodate our tastes and dietary requirements, was taught to me very early in our marriage by our friend Marion. Marion was and still is a fabulous cook. She's probably taught me more about cooking tasty food than anyone else in my life. Thank you, dear friend.

The recipe called for veal; however, the grocery stores here no longer sell veal. I have found thin-cut, boneless pork chops work very well, as would boneless, skinless chicken breast. Regardless of what you use, the meat needs to be pounded until very thin, which tenderizes it. My hands no longer have the strength to do it, so the butcher in the meat department graciously does it for me.

1 ¼-1 ½ pounds of meat for 4 servings, about 5-6 ounces per person. Figure accordingly, depending on the appetites in your family

2 large sweet onions, halved and sliced into semi-circle rings

1 box whole white mushrooms, sliced thinly

2-4 tablespoons olive oil

¼ cup flour

½ cup white dry wine

Ketchup

Salt, pepper, garlic powder, Italian seasoning (see Note)

1 tablespoon butter

1 tablespoon capers

Parmesan cheese, optional

Cut the pieces of pounded meat (pork, veal, or chicken) into 3-inch squares. Put flour and all seasonings into a produce bag, place meat pieces in, close bag, and shake to cover all pieces.

Heat 2 tablespoons oil in a large skillet and add the floured-seasoned meat pieces and brown on both sides. Do not crowd the pan, so do the meat in two batches. Remove meat to a bowl.

Add butter to the pan and sauté the onions, gathering all the meat juices from the bottom of the pan. Add mushrooms and cook. Add wine and a good squeeze of ketchup for color. Taste for seasoning and adjust.

Bring to low boil (simmer) and return meat to skillet. Cook, covered, on low, for 8-10 minutes. Sprinkle with capers and serve with Parmesan cheese if desired.

Four slices of the meat, along with onions and mushrooms, makes a great serving. Serve plain on the plate or over a bed of rice, along with a green salad or green vegetable.

Pork Chops

Since I can no longer eat chicken, pork chops have become my new "white meat." They are definitely not kosher.

This is technique, rather than a recipe. I have finally figured it out: How to Serve a Tender Pork Chop.

Preheat oven to 400º F.

Buy rib-cut thick pork chops, bone in. Season with salt, pepper, and garlic powder . Brown in hot skillet, 5 minutes per side.

Place skillet, if oven proof, in oven, or transfer chops to baking pan. Roast at 400º F for 20 minutes. Remove, cover with foil, and let rest for 10 minutes before serving.

While I'm pre heating the oven, I slice large potatoes (ten to twelve even slices), crosswise, season and oil them, and place on parchment paper on a baking sheet. I do the same for frozen broccoli florets and put them in the oven first as it's heating. Season and oil the broccoli when roasting.

When I put chops in the oven, I turn the potatoes over with a spatula and turn the broccoli over at the same time. Believe it or not, the vegetables take longer in the oven than the chops. After removing the chops and covering them, turn off oven and leave veggies in the oven to finish cooking for the 10 minutes that the pork chops are resting.

Just to clarify:

Preheat oven.

Add broccoli.

Cut and add potatoes.

Brown chops in pan on the stovetop.

Oven should be heated to 400º F by this time.

Add chops to oven. Turn vegetables.

Set timer for 20 minutes, remove and cover the chops.

Turn off oven and let veggies finish cooking.

Serve a delicious dinner.

Pork Chop with Green Beans and Sweet Potatoes

Baby Back Spareribs

I love making these — easy to make: just don't be in a hurry to eat.

I'm famous for my Baby Back Spareribs, or to paraphrase my husband, Jerry, "I'm a legend in my own mind."

The secret to spareribs is cooking them low and slow, whether in the oven or on the grill. My technique is pretty much the same for either method.

I usually make two racks of ribs when I make them since they take time and it's always more fun when sharing them with company.

Preheat oven to 300º F

Remove ribs from packaging and wash in the sink.

Cut each rack into two sections with each section having six ribs. Leave them in the sink and season them on both sides with a rub of your choice. I use salt, Montreal Steak seasoning (see Note), garlic powder, and a small amount of Grill Mates Rub (see Note), using whatever flavor Grill Mates is in the pantry.

Wrap the sections together in heavy duty foil, place in oven pans or on grill grates, and cook slowly at 300º F heat for 1 ½ hours, turning packages occasionally.

Remove from heat, cool, and unwrap ribs and place back in pans. When ready to serve, place in preheated 350º F oven to brown and sauce, maybe 15 minutes.

Always good and always tender.

Singapore Coffee Spareribs

A finger-licking Asian-style take on spareribs. You will love these.

We had these at a fabulous Dim Sum restaurant in San Francisco. They were so good, I needed to learn how to recreate them. The Internet... amazing stuff out there. These sound complicated to make but they're not, and they're so good.

Buy some pork or chicken potstickers and some pork or chicken soup dumplings (Trader Joe's) and create your own Dim Sum party.

One rack baby back ribs

Here's the secret: have your butcher slice the whole rack in half, lengthwise. At home, slice between the bones, into individual pieces, about 24 cubes, since the rib rack was cut lengthwise by the butcher.

Pork Seasoning:

½ teaspoon salt
2 tablespoons oyster sauce
1 teaspoon sesame oil
½ teaspoon baking soda
5 tablespoons corn starch
3 tablespoons water
1 egg, beaten
Oil, for deep frying

Sauce:

2 tablespoons instant coffee granules
3 tablespoons brown sugar
2 tablespoons white sugar
2 cloves garlic, finely minced
3 tablespoons BBQ sauce
1 tablespoon rice vinegar or wine
1 tablespoon soy sauce
5 tablespoons water

Cinnamon, ½ teaspoon

1 teaspoon chili flakes, optional

Preparation:

Mix all the pork seasoning ingredients together and toss with the pork rib cubes. Set aside and marinate in the refrigerator for 60 minutes.

After marinating, heat the oil in saucepan and deep fry the pork rib cubes until a deep golden color. Do not crowd the pan. Remove to a plate and fry the next batch.

Combine all the sauce ingredients in a large skillet and bring to a simmer. Reduce until the sauce thickens and thinly coats the back of a spoon.

Add the pork spare rib cubes to the pan and toss to coat evenly. Reduce further until sauce becomes a sticky glaze.

Note: It doesn't take very long to fry the rib cubes. To test them, I removed one when it was golden brown and cut into it. It was amazingly tender. I used a deep saucepan since I don't have a fryer, with maybe 3 inches of oil. This sounds complicated but it really isn't: just have all the seasoning ingredients together and while the pork is marinating, make the sauce and cook it partway, then reduce it and add the pork.

Put on platter and serve! Yum! And you don't have to go to San Francisco.

Singapore Coffee Spareribs

Linda's Singapore Coffee Spareribs

Hawaiian Kalua Pork

This is my favorite Hawaiian dish, and I make a reasonable facsimile. This is a technique, not a recipe.

I look for already cooked and pulled pork shoulder, not barbecue-sauced pork.

Sauté ½ head of cabbage and ½ a yellow onion, chopped, until brown and tender.

Add pulled pork and a little liquid smoke flavor (see Note): start with 1 teaspoon and taste. I like it smoky, so I use 1 tablespoon.

Serve over Asian sticky white rice.

It's a quick and easy trip to the Islands. Add a Mai Tai or some tropical punch, and relax and enjoy.

Sheet Pan Meals

I made my first sheet-pan meal after daughter Leslie shared a New England Boiled dinner, camp-out style.

Another new technique I've learned from AllRecipes.com is sheet pan cooking. Everything cooks on one parchment-covered sheet pan together and for the same amount of time, with a few exceptions. My favorite is this take-off on a New England boiled dinner.

Small potatoes, cut in half or quarters

Chunks of corn on the cob (or I'll just throw frozen corn kernels on the pan halfway through cooking)

1 onion, peeled and chunked.

Kielbasa sausage, cut in 2-inch pieces

4-5 shrimp per person

Your choice of seasonings (salt, pepper, paprika, garlic powder)

Preheat oven to 400º F.

Throw potatoes, onions, corn on cob, and sausage in the parchment-covered pan, and roast for 15 minutes.

Add shrimp and corn kernels (if not using corn on the cob). Return to oven. Check after 10 minutes and stir. If shrimp is cooked, remove and serve.

Variations: Throw a collection of veggies on the tray and roast. Broccoli, asparagus, cauliflower, carrots, Brussels sprouts, sweet potatoes, onions, and peppers all work.

Note: Allow extra time in oven for one crowded pan, or use two pans. You want the food to roast, not steam.

There are all sorts of meats and veggie combinations to try. Use your imagination and whatever you like. One pan, easy clean up, delicious dinner.

Sheet Pan Meal with Shrimp, Sausage, Corn, and Potatoes

Lamb Chops

Another easy meal we enjoyed was rib lamb chops. Very fast and savory.

There was a time when lamb was not as expensive a meat as it is now. The price has gone through the moon. Way back in the day, the butchers would package the lamb rib chops about 10-12 to a package and one package was enough for us with side dishes. They were always a treat. Granddaughter Sarah reminded me about these. Apparently, I used to make them more often than I do now.

I would place them on a broiler pan, season with salt, pepper, and garlic powder, and then put them under the broiler. Then flip them to cook the second side and serve. The trick was to watch them so they got brown and crisp but not burned.

Loin chops were bigger and meatier, but I didn't like them. The rib chops seemed less gamey tasting.

Rack of Lamb

I first made rack of lamb after ordering it in a "fancy" restaurant. When I made it, I was amazed at how easy it was to prepare.

Rack of lamb was always a fancy restaurant dish until I discovered the racks at Costco. One rack of eight bones would feed Jerry and me with leftovers for lunch the next day. Lamb is very rich and filling.

Preheat oven to 400º F.

Remove the lamb from the package and wash and dry it.

Season fat side up very heavily with salt, pepper, garlic powder, and Italian seasoning (see Note).

Brown fat side down in hot oven-proof skillet until very dark. Place skillet in 400º F oven for 15-20 minutes, depending on how you like to serve meat. Remove and cover with a foil tent to allow meat to rest. Cut through the bones and serve.

For company, I cut double chops since it makes a more elegant presentation, but for just us, I cut into single chops. Since the oven was on, I'd start oven-browned potatoes before the lamb rack so they'd cook and be ready to serve after the rack was sliced. Asparagus or broccoli make a tasty addition to the plate.

Desserts

Baking desserts is not something I do regularly, but I've learned a few delicious, mostly chocolate, desserts to make for holiday meals, usually for Passover.

Passover Meringue Drops

Loved by everyone, and so easy to make!

A good friend introduced me to these during Passover, and I fell in love with them. They're easy to make (since I don't bake!) and delicious.

2 egg whites
¾ cup sugar
1 teaspoon vanilla
6 ounces chocolate chips
½ cup chopped, toasted walnuts (see Note)

Preheat oven to 350º F.

Line 2 cookie sheets with foil.

Beat egg whites to soft stiff. Add vanilla and beat in. Gradually add sugar & continue beating until stiff.

Fold in chocolate chips and walnuts.

Drop mixture by teaspoons on cookie sheets, leaving space for expansion.

Put cookie sheets into oven at the same time and IMMEDIATELY turn off oven. Let sit in the oven for 3 hours: no peeking, and DO NOT open the oven door.

Remove Meringue Drops from cookie sheets and store in a cool, dry covered container.

Makes about 40 Meringues, 20 per cookie sheet.

Matzo Roca

Very simple to make and oh, so delish.

This recipe started out on the box of saltine crackers and was called "toffee." Someone in the Jewish community realized it could be adapted to matzo, and it became a Passover staple almost immediately. It was before the Internet, so it traveled the country by word of mouth, or as Jerry loved to call it, "The Coconut Wireless."

2-3 matzo sheets
1 cup butter
1 cup brown sugar
1 twelve-ounce package chocolate chips, milk or semisweet, your choice
4-5 ounces chopped or slivered almonds, toasted (see Note)
PAM cooking spray

Preheat oven to 350º F

Line cookie sheet with foil, dull side up. Spray foil with cooking spray. Lay squares of matzo flat on cookie sheet, breaking to fit and to cover pan.

In saucepan, melt butter and brown sugar, let boil on medium heat for 5 minutes, stirring constantly.

Pour mixture over matzo.

Bake for 5 minutes.

Remove from oven and immediately spread chocolate chips evenly over hot matzo until melted. Sprinkle almonds on top of melted chocolate. Add a very scant sprinkle of kosher salt over the pan. This brings out the flavor of the chocolate.

Freeze until hardened, and then break into pieces. Enjoy!

Variations: I usually make two pans; one with milk chocolate chips and one with semisweet. I made a pan once using craisins and pistachio nuts over the chocolate and it was delicious. I think I got that idea from Hadassah magazine. Use your imagination.

Matzo Roca

Rugelach

I've never met a rugelach I didn't like.

I have been told that I make great rugelach cookies so even though I haven't made them for ages, I'm including the recipe here. My secret is I use way too much sugar/cinnamon sprinkle on the dough, and I toast the chopped walnuts. I use golden raisins, but regular raisins or craisins (dried cranberries) are delicious. I prefer apricot jam, but any flavor works. That's the fun part (for me) of making rugelach: use your imagination to make any kind you want. Just follow the dough instructions because after all, it is baking.

Dough

1 cup (2 sticks) unsalted butter, softened
8 ounces cream cheese, softened
2 tablespoons sugar
¼ teaspoon salt
2 cups all-purpose flour

Beat together the butter, cream cheese, and sugar until light and fluffy. Add the salt, and gradually beat in the flour.

Divide into 4 equal portions, form into balls, wrap in Saran Wrap, and refrigerate overnight.

When ready to make rugelach, remove dough from refrigerator and let the dough stand at room temperature until workable.

Filling

1 cup finely chopped walnuts or pecans, lightly toasted (see Note)
½ cup raisins, dried currants, or craisins
½ cup granulated sugar
1 teaspoon cinnamon
1 cup apricot jam (or whatever flavor) you prefer

Preheat oven to 350º F.

To make the filling:

Combine the nuts, raisins, sugar, and cinnamon.

To make the Rugelach:

On lightly floured surface, roll out each dough ball, one at a time, into a ⅛-inch thick circle, about 15 inches in diameter.

Brush the dough rounds with jam leaving a ½-inch border around edge. Sprinkle evenly with filling mixture.

Cut each round into 12 or 16 wedges, depending on desired number and size. Roll up wedges from wide end toward point, pinching the point to seal. Gently bend to form crescents.

Make an egg wash with 1 egg beaten and brush the top of each crescent. Sprinkle lightly with extra sugar and cinnamon.

Bake at 350º F for 25 minutes until browned.

Cool completely before serving. Store in an airtight container if you have any leftovers.

Mandelbrot

Everyone's recipe is different, but mandelbrot is mandelbrot: it's all good.

These are the Jewish version of biscotti but are usually smaller and more thinly sliced. Every Jewish baker makes them slightly differently, but this is a basic recipe. You want chocolate, throw in some mini chips; orange flavor, add a little juice or zest. Don't be afraid of all the oil and sugar; this makes four loaves which get cut into 12-16 slices each.

1 cup corn or vegetable oil
1 cup sugar
4 eggs
1 teaspoon vanilla
1-2 drops almond extract
4 cups all-purpose or gluten-free flour
1 teaspoon baking powder, heaping
Salt, a pinch
1 cup slivered almonds

For Topping:

½ cup sugar
½ teaspoon cinnamon
(combine sugar and cinnamon)

Preheat oven to 350º F.

Cream together oil and sugar. Add eggs one at a time, beating each one in. Add vanilla and almond extract.

Sift together the flour, baking powder, and salt. Add to the sugar and egg mixture.

Stir in 1 cup slivered almonds.

Shape the dough into long loaves on greased cookie sheets, 2 loaves to a sheet. Sprinkle tops of loaves with sugar and cinnamon mixture.

Bake at 350º F for 30 minutes or until browned.

When done, remove from oven, turn oven off, and close door. Slice the loaves immediately at an angle, turn each piece sideways, and place back in oven for a few minutes until the pieces become crisp slices.

Store in an airtight container.

Aunt Linda's Pecan Caramel Candies (Turtles)

The name of these in a magazine attracted me to check it out. So I made them.

The recipe is on the bag of Rolo candies, but I like calling it "Aunt Linda's Turtles."

Mini pretzel twists (one pretzel for each candy)
1 bag Rolo candies (in the candy aisle of your grocer)
Pecan halves (one for each candy)

Preheat oven to 250º F.

Line a baking sheet with foil. Place pretzels 1 inch apart on foil. Put 1 Rolo centered on top of each pretzel. Bake 3-4 minutes or until candy is softened but not melted.

Remove from oven and quickly press a pecan half onto each Rolo, pushing down gently so the candy spreads into the pretzel.

Let stand until set, and then share.

The hardest job in this process is unwrapping each of the Rolo candies. It's a perfect job for little fingers if you have any kids around.

Aunt Linda's Pecan Caramel Candies (Turtles)

Mexican Wedding Cookies

I don't know why these are not called Jewish Wedding Cookies,
but by any other name, they really are good.

Jerry loves these cookies, and occasionally I would make them for him, but that was long after Caren, Rachel, and Leslie had all graduated college. I don't remember ever baking cookies with my children, so I guess I cheated them out of a childhood experience that every child should have; however, they have all turned out great so I guess I didn't scar them for life.

One year when Leslie was home on winter break from college, the two of us went to my dear friend Myrna's (May her memory be a blessing) to help her make us a batch of Mexican Wedding Cookies. During the afternoon, Leslie commented that it was the first time she had ever baked cookies with her mom (me), and Myrna was aghast. What kind of a mother was I? We still laugh about that.

These cookies are easy to make, and the recipe is available very readily on the Internet, but I will include it here. They are also known as Italian Wedding Cookies or snowball cookies. Try them! You'll love them!

And make them with your children so they won't feel deprived of a childhood experience.

---

1 cup unsalted butter
½ cup white sugar
2 teaspoons vanilla
2 teaspoons water
2 cups all-purpose flour
1 cup finely chopped nuts: walnuts, pecans, or almonds
¼ teaspoon salt

Beat butter and sugar until light and fluffy. Add vanilla and water. Beat until combined. Add flour, nuts, and salt. Beat until combined

Cover and chill for 2 hours.

Preheat oven to 325º F.

Shape chilled dough into 1 inch balls and put on ungreased cookie sheets.

Bake 15-20 minutes. Note: they won't be browned.

Remove and cool slightly on racks.

Place powdered sugar in bowl and roll warm cookies to coat. Roll the cookies in the powdered sugar a second time.

Store in an airtight container at room temperature.

Our granddaughter Anya makes these, gluten free, and they're just as delicious. In fact, they're more than yummy, because she makes them and shares them with us. And everything she makes is gluten free, so all her desserts can be served for Passover.

One word of advice: don't breathe in as you're taking a bite of these cookies. The powdered sugar will get all over your clothes and may cause a coughing fit.

Apple Latkes

These make for a different Chanukah treat.
They're not donuts but they meet the requirement for Chanukah: they're fried.

This is another one of Marion's recipes and like most of hers, the latkes require some work, but they are delicious. I was visiting her in December one year, and she hosted a Chanukah party. My job was to fry these latkes and sugar them. Her friends' appetites were insatiable, and I spent the evening frying battered apple slices. They really are delicious, though, and worth the work.

6-8 tart apples, green or Pippin
1 ½ tablespoons cinnamon
1 cup sugar, mixed with the cinnamon
Oil for frying

Batter:

3 eggs
1 cup milk
1 teaspoon vegetable oil
1 ½ cups flour

Pare, core, and slice apples, ⅓-inch thick.

Preheat oven to 350º F.

Combine all batter ingredients in blender and blend until smooth.

Dip apple slices in batter and fry in hot oil in a large skillet. Do not overcrowd the pan. Fry apple slices until brown on both sides, turning once.

Place the fried apple slices on a cookie sheet lined with parchment paper; sprinkle with cinnamon/sugar mixture, turn, and sprinkle the other side with the cinnamon-sugar mixture.

Place in 350º F oven for 10-12 minutes, until crispy brown.

Serve and enjoy. Serves 8.

Peach Crisp

I make these as a labor of love, because using homegrown juicy peaches is beyond words.

These I make from the peaches from our own tree, so come July and August, I'm busy making this dessert. I discovered they can be frozen uncooked, so now I make a double batch in 8 ramekins and freeze 4. When I take them out of the freezer, I bake them and we eat them, and then I do it again: 4 fresh, 4 frozen, and then I do another batch. It keeps me busy for the month of the peaches, and then I'm done.

Filling

Fresh peaches, approximately 2 large or 3 small, for each ramekin
Cinnamon
Brown sugar

Topping, for 4 ramekins (see Note)

½ cup quick oatmeal
½ cup flour
½ cup cold butter, cut into pieces
½ cup brown sugar
½ teaspoon cinnamon
Pinch of salt

Preheat oven to 350º F.

To make the filling:

Cut each peach in half, remove pit, and peel peaches. Cut into large pieces and sprinkle with cinnamon and brown sugar. Divide peaches into four ramekins, filling each almost to the top, leaving some room to cover with crisp topping.

To make the topping:

Mix ingredients for topping well by hand in a bowl and crumble together until the butter coats the topping and everything is mixed.

Cover tops of peach-filled ramekins with topping. Bake on cookie sheet covered with foil for ½ hour at 350º F. They should be brown on top and bubbly.

Note: If I'm doing 8 ramekins, or I'm making it in an 8x8 baking dish, I double the topping recipe.

Variation: I have made these crisps with apples, and they're delicious, too.

Peach Crisp

Award-winning Peaches

Cherry Blossom Dessert

Silly name, but a delightful treat just the same.

My mom, Bamma Freda, made a great dessert with canned cherries that she called "Cherry Blossom Dessert." It called for a crust on the bottom, then the filling, and then a crisp mixture topping. Her recipe is from the 1950s, and I include it here so it isn't lost. What I find most interesting is that 70 years later, it's a crisp recipe with a different name.

My mom's recipe did not include baking the bottom layer first, but I explicitly remember her doing that, so I've included it in the recipe.

Filling:

1 can sour pitted cherries, drained, with juice set aside
¼ cup all-purpose flour
1 cup sugar
¾ cup cherry juice from the can of sour pitted cherries
1 tablespoon butter
Juice of ½ lemon
Pinch of salt
½ teaspoon almond extract

Crust and Topping:

1 ½ cups all-purpose flour
1 teaspoon salt
1 teaspoon baking soda
1 cup brown sugar
1 cup quick oatmeal
½ cup cold butter, cut into pieces

Preheat oven to 350º F

To make the filling:

Combine the flour, sugar, and cherry juice in a saucepan and cook until thick. When thickened, add the sour pitted cherries. Let cool until warm, then add the butter, lemon juice, salt, and almond extract.

To make the crisp base and topping:

Blend together in a bowl, the flour, salt, baking soda, brown sugar, and oatmeal. Cut the butter into the dry mixture.

Press ½ of the crust mixture into the bottom of an ungreased square pan (8x8" or 9x9"), and bake the crust at 350º F for 10 minutes to set. Remove from oven and cool completely.

Spread with cooled cherry filling. Top with remaining oatmeal mixture and bake at 350º F for 25-30 minutes until bubbly.

Cool to room temperature, cut into squares and serve with whipped cream or ice cream.

Variation: As an afterthought, since I was always looking for shortcuts, I would buy a can of cherry pie filling and add a squeeze of lemon juice when I made this, and I thought it tasted the same as the more complex filling. Then I'd make the topping mixture, and Jerry always loved it. In fact, I just might make it again.

Grandma Adele's Orange Cake

This cake has fruit, nuts, and booze. What could be bad?

This is a recipe of Grandma Adele's and I actually made it a few times for Jerry early in our marriage. He told me it wasn't like his mother's and so, since I'm not a baker, I never made it again. I have to admit that it was pretty good. The sauce that gets spooned over the cake when it's done was delicious: one could get "sauced" while sampling it.

Be sure to read through the entire recipe and have all ingredients ready to go before starting.

Sauce:

½ cup sugar
2 tablespoons whiskey or brandy
Juice of 1 orange

Mix together all sauce ingredients in saucepan. Heat to lukewarm and stir until sugar is dissolved. Set aside.

Cake:

1 ½ cups sugar
1 cup butter
2 eggs
2 cups flour
1 teaspoon baking soda
Pinch salt
1 cup raisins
1 teaspoon vanilla
½ cup chopped walnuts
Juice and zest of one orange
2 tablespoons brandy or whiskey

Preheat oven to 350º F.

Cream together sugar and butter. Add the eggs. Beat well.

Sift the flour with the baking soda and salt. Add flour mixture to the creamed sugar mixture alternating with juice and zest of 1 orange, 2 tablespoons whiskey or brandy.

Add raisins, vanilla, and chopped walnuts. Pour batter into a greased and floured tube pan.

Bake at 350º F for one hour.

Let cake cool for about 5 minutes and then, while still hot and in pan, spoon the sauce very gradually over the cake.

Chocolate Cake

Jerry remembers having this often growing up.
It was very dense and moist, almost like a brownie.

This was Jerry's Aunt Ruth Trachtenberg's famous chocolate cake. This Aunt Ruth, not to be confused with Aunt Ruthie Carsman, was Grandpa Morrie's only sister and they lived in San Bernardino. Here's her cake recipe (read about Aunt Ruth in the family history section earlier in this book).

½ cup shortening (see Note)
1 ½ cups sugar
3 eggs
2 squares chocolate, melted and cooled
1 ½ cups all-purpose flour
1 teaspoon baking soda
1 cup buttermilk
1 teaspoon vanilla

Preheat oven to 325º F.

Cream together shortening (or shortening substitute) and sugar. Add two eggs and beat well. Add melted and cooled chocolate. Blend well.

In a separate bowl, sift together the flour and baking soda. Add to the creamed mixture, alternating with buttermilk. Mix well. Add vanilla. Blend well.

Pour batter into two 9-inch layer floured pans. Bake at 325º F until tested done, 35-40 minutes. Let cool and add your favorite frosting.

Grandma Adele's Apple Cookies (sort of)

These are the most time-consuming cookies to make, but husband Jerry thinks they're worth it because he loves eating them.

I remember making apple cookies with Grandma Adele when Jerry and I were first married. It was a time-consuming, never-ending process. She made her own apple filling, but the few times I made the cookies, I used canned apple pie filling. She made the dough, rolled it out, and, using a glass, cut circles out in the dough. Then a small spoonful of apple filling went on ½ of a circle, then the circle was folded in half, sealed around the edge with water and then, using a fork, sealed again with the fork tines. It was very labor intensive and after doing one round of dough, I thought we were finished. Oh, no! We were just getting started. She gathered all the dough scraps from the first circle cutting, rolled it out again, and made more cookies. Then again and again until only one tiny bit of dough was left and from that, she made the last cookie. While they were baking, we started on the next large round of dough and redid the whole process. I'm guessing we made about 36 cookies which Jerry and his brother, Mel, proceeded to eat in one afternoon. I think I made the cookies once more on my own and that was that. Too much work... As a result of that experience, I decided baking was just not for me.

Leslie and I tried them once using a Hamentashen (tri-cornered cookies made specifically for Purim) dough and they were good but Grandma Adele's dough recipe was softer and more pliable. I'm thinking it might have been like a pie dough recipe. (Leslie, it's worth a try...).

Grandma Adele's Apple Cookies (sort of)

A Little Jewish History and Food

Jewish foods have always been part of the history of the Jews. Wherever they moved in exile, they adapted their lifestyles and foods to their new lands and to what was available to them. Holidays celebrate the past, and some holidays require traditional and ritual meals: matzo on Passover, fried foods on Chanukah, and sweet foods on Rosh Hashanah for a good sweet year.

When the Jews were banished by the Romans from Jerusalem, they spread out into two important Jewish communities. Some went to Iberia (Spain) and some to the Rhine River Valley (Europe.) Those who went to Iberia, ruled by Muslims, were called the Sephardim, and believe it or not, lived in relative harmony with the Muslims and often held positions of influence. Those who moved to Europe were the Ashkenazi, and they had to live apart from the generally hostile Christian population in the lands of Europe. There are other ethnic Jewish groups but the Sephardic and Ashkenazi are the main ones.

The Sephardic Jewish community in Spain, who lived there for many centuries, were forced to move or convert to Christianity during the Spanish Inquisition at the end of the 15th century. In 1492, the remaining Jews in Spain were expelled, and they scattered back to the Middle East, or to North Africa, Mediterranean Europe, and the New World. Do you remember the mnemonic? "In 1492, Columbus sailed the ocean blue." Coincidence? Who knows?

The Ashkenazi, who lived in the Rhine Valley for centuries, spread to France, Italy, and Germany as they grew more numerous. In the 11th century, the Christian Crusaders pushed the Jews further east into Poland and other Eastern European areas. The Pale of Settlement, then part of Russia but later conquered by other countries, was where many of the Jews were restricted to live.

Each community, the Sephardic and the Ashkenazi, adapted their diets and food traditions to what was available to them. The Sephardic used the spices, herbs, and foods of the Mediterranean: olive oil, fish, lamb, fruits, and vegetables. The Ashkenazi food was cold-climate food. They pickled cabbage into sauerkraut, and cucumbers into pickles; made dumplings to distribute very little meat among more people; and adapted to potatoes when introduced to them.

Since I grew up in an Ashkenazi family, "soul" foods for me are Deli foods: rye bread, pastrami, pickles, bean and barley soup, split pea soup, matzo ball soup and rugelach.

A dear friend of ours, Sarah Wargo, loved to cook and we used to stay in a time-share unit together when her husband, Joe, and Jerry attended trade shows together. One time, Sarah made *kibbeh*, a Sephardic dumpling made of pounded bulgur wheat and ground beef, and she was so proud of herself for making Jewish food for us. We had never tasted it, and I think it's an acquired taste, sort of how gefilte fish is an acquired taste. She couldn't understand how we didn't know about *kibbeh*. She's from Brazil and is not Jewish but was familiar with it as a Jewish food in Brazil. So, there you go: two totally different Jewish communities and food traditions.

In recent years, I've become much more interested in Israeli cuisine and spices and flavors, but I haven't ventured into the actual cooking of Sephardic dishes. I enjoy going to Middle Eastern and Mediterranean restaurants and sampling the menu. The vegetable choices are generally delicious and plentiful, and it's interesting to realize I'm eating Jewish foods that have been part of the diets of Jews for centuries.

Definitely not my Jewish heritage and foods, but Jewish food regardless. I've been a foodie all my life, and it's incredibly interesting, now at my age, to realize that Jewish foods are what has kept our heritage alive.

A Glossary of Jewish Cooking Phrases

B'tay Ah Vone (Hebrew) translates to "Good Appetite" or "Eat with Good Appetite"

Fress (Yiddish) To eat or to snack, copiously and without restraint

Nosh (Yiddish) To snack; also, a light meal or a snack

Potchke (Yiddish) To fuss or mess around, usually in the kitchen, as in, " I was potchke-ing around in the kitchen when I came up with this new dish"

So, to all my readers, I wish for you a lifetime of *fressing, noshing, potchke-ing,* and good appetite. *B'tay Ah Vone...*

Typical (or not) Holiday Meals

Every family has their own style and special foods that represent the Jewish Holidays to them. These ideas are merely suggestions, however; whatever works for your family and your tastes becomes your holiday meal.

The past few years, with no little ones at our Passover *Seder* table anymore, we've begun to change our own customs. I still prepare the *Seder* Plate for the table, including an orange on the plate. Many years ago, but within recent history, an old-fashioned Rabbi, angry that women were being considered for rabbinical schools and serving as fully ordained Rabbis, decreed that women belonged in rabbinical schools like oranges belonged on the *Seder* Plate. As the mother of three daughters, that did not resonate well with me, and an orange has been on my *Seder* Plate ever since. And, women are doing a fabulous job within the Reform, Reconstructionist, and Conservative Jewish communities. More recently, an orange on the *Seder* Plate has come to symbolize solidarity with marginalized communities.

Passover Wine Tasting

The Passover *Seder* mandates drinking four cups of wine during the *Seder.* In our family, this is not a problem, so the past few *Seders,* we have turned our cups of wine into a blind wine-tasting. Jerry picks a designated varietal of wine, every family unit brings a bottle of the chosen varietal. Then they get opened and I bag each bottle, rubber band the bags to the tops, and mix and change positions of the bottles and randomly number the bags. We each get a wine ranking paper with scores from 5 to 1, with 5 as the best to our taste and 1 as the worst. We start tasting with bottle #1, rank it, dump or drink it, and move on to the next bottle until we've tasted and ranked each wine. We unwrap the bottles to see who brought the table's wines. Bragging rights count for a lot. Everyone partakes of their favorite during dinner and a lively time is enjoyed by all. Of course, there's always Manischewitz and non-alcoholic beverages available.

A friend recently told me they did a Japanese food *Seder* dinner with Sushi subbing for gefilte fish, roasted salmon as their main, and lots of veggie dishes with mochi ice cream as their dessert. Very creative, and they all had a great meal. So, use your imagination, travel the world, and have fun at the Seder.

Here's a brief overview of the Jewish Holidays and my interpretation of typical meals.

Shabbat (The Sabbath)

Shabbat (the Sabbath) may be one of Judaism's greatest gifts to the world. The idea of "a day to rest" changed the quality of life for so many people. The Jewish Sabbath is Saturday, so that means sundown on Friday night begins *Shabbat.* All Jewish holidays, including *Shabbat,* begin at sundown the night before so be sure to note this on your calendar.

Many people attend Friday night services at their Temple or Synagogue and/or *Shabbat* morning services on Saturday. *Shabbat* ends traditionally at sundown on Saturday with the *Havdalah* service which closes *Shabbat* and welcomes the new week.

A typical *Shabbat* meal:
Kosher Wine
Challah
Soup (bean & barley or chicken)
Roasted chicken
Rice
Green beans (or any other vegetable)
Cake (or any dessert)

Rosh Hashanah (The New Year)

We pray for a good and sweet New Year with our thoughts on the year that has passed and the new one about to begin. The challah is usually round and made with raisins to symbolize continuity, and sliced apples and honey are served for a good sweet year.

A *Rosh Hashanah* meal:
Chopped liver (or veggie "mock" dip)
Soup (chicken or cabbage)
Brisket
Green vegetable
Oven roasted potatoes
Apple or honey cake

Yom Kippur (The Day of Atonement)

This is the most solemn day of the year; a day of reflection and prayer. It is customary to fast on *Yom Kippur* providing your health allows it. The break-the-fast meal is a simple one with dairy foods, smoked fish, and other light tidbits, and always Jewish baked goods.

A *Yom Kippur* meal:
Hummus and pita chips
Bagels, lox, and cream cheese

Smoked white fish or herring
Blintzes
Noodle Pudding
Mandelbrot or other cookies

Sukkot (The Festival of Booths)

Sukkot is two weeks after *Rosh Hashanah* and honors the small booths the Israelites built as they wandered during their time in the desert. A *Sukkah* is a temporary structure built by families outdoors, and meals are eaten in the *Sukkah.* Its roof is palm branches (where available), and it's decorated with drawings or photos of fruit and vegetables. Do not use real fruit and vegetables; our Temple did that once and it was a disaster as the weather turned very hot: think bugs...

A *Sukkot* meal:
Vegetable soup
Green salad with mandarin oranges
Beef Stew
Buttered noodles
Date nut squares or Zucchini bread

Chanukah (The Festival of Lights)

Chanukah is an eight-day festival that commemorates the victory of the Jewish Maccabees over the Greek-Syrian army over 2,000 years ago. The Temple was re-dedicated and although only one small vial of oil was found, it lasted eight full days until more sacred oil was delivered. Thus we celebrate for eight days and eat fried foods.

Ashkenazi Jews generally serve latkes (potato pancakes), and Israeli Jews eat fried jelly donuts called *Sufganiyot.*

A *Chanukah* meal:
Marinated Flank Steak or Tri-tip Roast
Potato Latkes
Carrots or Roasted Broccoli
Apple Sauce
Sour Cream
Sufganiyot or Fried Apple Latkes

Tu B'Shvat (New Year of the Trees)

"And they shall sit every man under his vine and under his fig tree,
and none shall make them afraid." ~ *Micah 4:4*

When the Israelites finished wandering for 40 years, they returned to their homeland. God told them to plant trees, and to grow fruit, vegetables, and grains. Today, a tree is usually planted at the Temple or Synagogue or, with permission, in a park or on private land by religious school children. Sometimes a different *Seder* is held where you eat fruits, nuts, vegetables, and carob and honey snacks.

A *Tu B'Shvat Seder*
French Bread or Wheat Crackers
Vegetable Spread
Vegetable or Minestrone Soup
Vegetable Lasagna
Cookies
Seder Plate with Figs, Dates, Raisins, Carob, Almonds, Olives, and Pomegranates

Purim (The Feast of Esther)

Purim is a Spring holiday celebrating Queen Esther and her Uncle Mordecai for saving the Jewish people from the wicked Haman. Temples and Synagogues celebrate this holiday with lots of costumes, music, masks, food, drink, noise-makers, and dancing. Three cornered filled pastries called *Hamentashen* (Haman's ear) are baked and served.

There is no special menu or special foods for *Purim:* just a quick dinner and then off to the Temple or Synagogue for the *Purim* Festival.

A fairly new custom are *Shalach Manot* baskets which are made available to all members of the congregation and contain *Hamentashen,* Rugelach, mixed nuts, dried fruits, and chocolate. It's a fun gift for all.

Pesach (Passover: The Feast of Freedom)

This holiday commemorates the freeing of the Israelites from being slaves to Pharaoh and Egypt. Led by Moses, the Jews fled so quickly that their bread could not rise, thus the matzo that is eaten for eight days. No leavened bread is served during Passover.

We tell and retell the story of Passover every year with all of the ritual foods and customs that we adopted or grew up with.

The table has the traditional Passover *Seder* Plate, and as we read the prayers, drink the wine, and tell the story, we partake in or discuss the significance of the Egg, Shank Bone, Bitter Herbs, Parsley, Horseradish and Charoseth, the Matzo, and the Four Cups of Wine. Then the meal is served.

Carsman Family Passover Table, 2024

A *Pesach* (Passover) Menu:
Gefilte Fish
Matzo Ball Soup
Brisket
Potato or Matzo Kugel

Carrots and/or Sweet Potato
Passover Chocolate Torte or Flourless Chocolate Cake
Macaroons
Meringue Drops
Matzo Roca

Carsman Passover Dinner 2024: Brisket, Roasted Potatoes, and Charred Broccoli

Not all these desserts are served. These are just ideas: my family doesn't like coconut, so macaroons are never served. I make the Matzo Roca, and granddaughter Anya usually makes one of her delicious non-dairy, gluten-free desserts. This year, we had the Matzo Roca and her non-dairy, gluten-free cheesecake with homemade raspberry sauce. Delicious! Obviously, we do not keep kosher, but we do try to follow the rules and rituals of Passover. There will never be bread on the Passover table, but as stated earlier in this chapter, there is an orange on the Seder Plate.

Shavuot (The Giving of the Torah)

Immediately following the Passover *Seder,* the Jewish people count seven weeks (or 49 days) until the date they were given the Torah on Mount Sinai. This date is called *Shavuot*, the Festival of the Giving of the Torah.

Dairy foods are traditionally served since once the Torah was given, there was no more mixing of dairy and meat products to keep kosher.

Customs evolved around the world but for Ashkenazi Jews, cheesecake, cheese blintzes, cheese kreplach, dairy filled noodle kugel, and cheese ravioli are served. Fresh fruits of the season are also served.

Look up any Jewish holiday on the Internet for further suggestions and/or holiday recipes. Every family has their own traditions. Experiment and create your own. Dietary restrictions? Research and find recipes you can pass down to your children and grandchildren. Enjoy!

So, to all my readers, I wish for you a lifetime of *fressing, noshing, potchke-ing,* and good appetite. *B'tay Ah Vone...*

Handy Hints

New Tricks:

Contrary to what they say, an old gal can always learn new tricks.

When recuperating from my knee surgeries, watching Rachael Ray's "30 Minute Meals," I learned about using a "garbage bowl" in the sink for peels, onion skins, veggie ends, etc. Wonderful idea and I've refined it even further. I now use a plastic produce bag that I bring my vegetables home in from the grocery store. I fold it in half, fill it with the cooking refuse, and then knot it and throw it in the freezer until garbage day. No additional dirty dishes to wash and nothing stinky in the garbage.

Another tip I learned from her show was to use the largest wooden cutting board that would fit on the counter. What a difference a large cutting board makes. No more small boards for me and none of the plastic ones either. I acknowledge that I don't cook chicken, so I don't worry about the necessity of not contaminating the cutting board. I clean my wood cutting boards regularly and then rub lemon juice on it, and I've not ever poisoned anyone with my food prep or cooking.

My large board is 18x24 inches and holds a lot of piles of cut up meats, veggies, and salad greens. The other board I use is for cutting breads and other pastries and is 10x17 inches. It was made by a friend who loves woodworking and donates these to our congregation as a fundraiser.

Since baking is precise, try to have all the necessary ingredients on hand; however, if you're going to use any substitutions, keep the measurements accurate.

Cutting Boards

Cooking is different: experiment with different flavors and spices. Jerry says he hates garlic, but I've discovered that it's fresh garlic he doesn't like. I use garlic powder, and he's fine with that. When I'm just starting to sauté onions, which he loves on or in anything, and I've sprinkled garlic powder on the onions, he wanders into the kitchen to tell me that "something smells delicious." It's hardly started cooking, but that fragrance gets him every time. Just like with real garlic, don't let the garlic powder burn. It does get bitter, so add your liquid or sauce to the pan before it burns.

With today's high prices for food, buying tougher cuts of meats and braising (roasted in a covered pan with liquid) them is an easy way to cook for a couple or a family. I don't have a slow cooker, but they're perfect for these kinds of meals. I had one of the very first slow cookers, but it couldn't be submerged in water for thorough cleaning, so I eventually tossed it out when we moved to our current house, 25 years ago. If you've got one, use it. I'm sure it's a godsend for working people and families.

I don't measure seasonings: I do a pinch of this, a couple of shakes of that, and I do a lot of tasting. I try not to over-season, especially salt. You can't un-salt, but you can always add salt if your tastebuds say a dish needs more. Because I watch our salt intake, I've gotten used to using less and less. I buy low-sodium or no-salt broths because I can then control the sodium. Salt-free V-8 vegetable juice has become a favorite to drink and use in cooking. Let your tastebuds be your guide.

A note on salt: I use less and less salt these days for health reasons, but what I use and always have used is Kosher salt with the coarsest grain I can find. I keep it in a little Pyrex cup in my seasoning cabinet and reach in for a tiny pinch whenever I need it.

There are so many wonderful magazines and sites that give information on cooking or baking substitutions when you don't have all the necessary ingredients: some of my favorites are All Recipes, Food Network, The Old Farmer's Almanac, and Betty Crocker.

Other Hints, Tricks, and Substitutions:

Beef Bouillon: Please be aware that some brands of beef bouillon contain ingredients which may be triggers for people with migraine, epilepsy, seizures, etc. Savory Suitcase and Glenda Embree offer recipes to substitute homemade bouillon for store-bought bouillon.

Beef Stew Seasoning Mix: There are various beef stew seasoning mixes on the market, and many contain gluten, soy, modified food starch, and/or maltodextrin, which can be triggers for people with migraine, celiac disease, seizure disorders, or other health issues. You can find various recipes that do not contain these items to help you easily make your own beef stew seasoning mix, including those from Rachel Cooks, Bake It with Love, and Food.com.

Cream of Chicken Soup: If you don't have cream of chicken soup on hand, you can make your own with a few ingredients, with this recipe from Tastes Better from Scratch. If you prefer using cream of mushroom soup but don't have any available, you can make your own with this recipe from Buns In My Oven.

Grill Mates Rub: There are various Grill Mates Rub mixes, but some of them — including the one for pork — contain maltodextrin, an additive which can be a trigger for people with migraine or other health issues. You can find various recipes that do not contain these items to help you easily make your own rub for the chops, including those from Hey, Grill, Hey, Vindulge, and The Cookie Rookie.

Heinz Savory Beef Gravy: Heinz Savory Beef Gravy contains modified food starch, maltodextrin, wheat flour, caramel color, and soy sauce, some of which may be triggers for those with migraine, celiac disease, seizure disorders, etc. To make your own substitute, see one of the recipes at Favorite Family Recipes, Creme de la Crumb, or The Slow Roasted Italian.

Italian Seasoning: If you don't have any Italian seasoning on hand, you can make your own with a few spices and herbs. Easy recipes can be found at Gimme Some Oven, The Mediterranean Dish, and All Recipes.

Lipton Onion Soup Mix: Lipton Onion Soup Mix contains MSG, caramel color, and other ingredients that may trigger migraines or seizures in sensitive people. If you don't have any Lipton soup mix or simply want to avoid those ingredients, you can make your own onion soup mix with recipes from Better from Scratch, Fountain Avenue Kitchen, or Food.com.

Liquid Smoke: If you don't have any liquid smoke, you can substitute a variety of spices and/or techniques. See suggestions at Pantry and Larder, Cozy Meal, and Corrie Cooks.

Mexican Cheese Blend: There are various Mexican cheese mixes on the market, and many contain gluten, soy, modified food starch, and/or maltodextrin, which can be triggers for people with migraine, seizure disorders, or other health issues. There are different cheeses in these mixes, including combinations of Monterey Jack, Cheddar, Colby, Asadero, Queso Quesadilla, etc. You can find various recipes that do not contain preservatives, artificial sweeteners, or flavor enhancers, etc. to help you easily make your own Mexican cheese mix, including those from Izzy Cooking, Eat Better, Spend Less, and Just a Pinch.

Montreal Steak Seasoning: If you don't have any Montreal Steak Seasoning, you can easily make your own with one of the recipes from Culinary Hill, Hey, Grill, Hey, or The Spruce Eats.

Potato Pancake Mix Ingredients:

Manischewitz Potato Pancake Mix ingredients: dehydrated potatoes, sulfites, sodium acid pyrophosphate, monoglycerides, potato starch, salt, onion, palm oil.

Streit's Potato Pancake Mix ingredients (New formula: no sulfites): potatoes, mono 7 diglycerides, sodium acid pyrophosphates, potato starch, onions, salt, olive oil.

Poultry Seasoning: If you don't have any poultry seasoning in the cupboard, you can make your own with a few herbs. Easy recipes can be found at All Recipes, Spend with Pennies, and Sweet and Savory Meals.

Shortening: Shortening can contain beef tallow, soybean oil, coconut oil, and/or palm oil. Please be sure to read ingredients carefully if you have concerns about ingredients and allergens. If you don't have any shortening or don't wish to use it, you can substitute other ingredients, many of which are listed in these articles by Food 52 or Food Network, which consider the recipe you're using, e.g., pie crust, biscuits, icing, bread, etc., when suggesting substitutions.

Taco Seasoning: There are various taco seasoning mixes on the market, and many contain gluten, soy, modified food starch, maltodextrin, milk, and bisulfites, which can be triggers for people with certain health issues. You can find various recipes that do not contain these items to help you easily make your own taco seasoning mix, including those from All Recipes, Love and Lemons, and Natasha's Kitchen.

Toasting Nuts: Toast walnuts, pecans, or other nuts in the microwave by putting nuts on a plate and microwave them for 3 minutes. Remove and stir them. Put back in microwave for a couple more minutes, remove again, and stir. Keep doing this until toasted. Times differ based on amount of nuts.

Worcestershire Sauce: According to *Food 52,* "Worcestershire gets its unique flavor from a combination of vinegar, molasses, anchovies, garlic, tamarind extract, chili pepper extract, sugar, and salt, along with other undisclosed 'natural ingredients' (which purportedly include cloves, soy, essence of lemons, and pickles)." Those with food intolerance or allergies to any of these ingredients should be aware of this. The article also contains substitutions for Worcestershire sauce.

Enough of my musings.

Measurements

Let's talk measurements... it's math, I know, but very important for baking. Cooking? Not so much but it helps to know approximately how much equals "whatever" you're measuring when you're cooking. Let's do the math:

Liquid Conversions:

¼ Cup = 2 fluid ounces
4 tablespoons
12 teaspoons
60 ml

½ Cup = 4 fluid ounces
8 tablespoons
24 teaspoons
120 ml

1 Cup = 8 fluid ounces
16 tablespoons
48 teaspoons (but who's going to do that?)
240 ml

1 Pint = 2 Cups
16 fluid ounces
470 ml, not 480 ml
It's crazy and that's why I don't use milliliters if I can help it. It turns out there's really only 59 ml in a ¼ cup, but it gets rounded up, so as the math gets higher, it needs to be rounded down for more accuracy Phew! Just go with it.

1 Quart = 2 pints
4 cups
32 fluid ounces
946 ml

1 Gallon = 4 quarts
8 pints
16 cups
128 fluid ounces
3.8 liters

Unless you're buying soda, wine, or liquor, milliliters or liters don't mean much to us living in the United States. In Europe, the metric system is what is used for baking and cooking.

Liquid Volumes:

1 teaspoon = 5 ml
1 tablespoon = 15 ml
Dash = 1⁄16 teaspoon
Pinch = ⅛ teaspoon

1 ounce = 6 teaspoons = 2 tablespoons = 30 ml
2 ounces = 12 teaspoons = 4 tablespoons = 60 ml
4 ounces = 24 teaspoons = 8 tablespoons = 120 ml
6 ounces = 36 teaspoons = 12 tablespoons = 177 ml
8 ounces = 48 teaspoons = 16 tablespoons = 240 ml
16 ounces = 96 teaspoons = 32 tablespoons = 470 ml
32 ounces= 192 teaspoons = 64 teaspoons = 950 ml

Dry Weights:

½ ounce = 1 tablespoon = 1⁄16 cup = 15 grams
1 ounce = 2 tablespoons = ⅛ cup = 28 grams
2 ounces = 4 tablespoons = ¼ cup = 57 grams
3 ounces = 6 tablespoons = ⅓ cup = 85 grams
4 ounces = 8 tablespoons = ½ cup = 115 grams = ¼ pound
8 ounces = 16 tablespoons = 1 cup = 227 grams = ½ pound
12 ounces = 24 tablespoons = 1-½ cups = 340 grams = ¾ pound
16 ounces = 32 tablespoons = 2 cups = 455 grams = 1 pound

Food Type Temperature of Doneness:

Fresh Beef, Veal and Lamb
(Steaks, Roasts & Chops) 145º F

Chicken, Turkey, Duck 165º F
(Pieces, Ground, Stuffing, Whole)

Non-Poultry Meat Mixtures
(Sausages, Loafs, Burgers) 160º F

Fresh Pork and Ham 145º F

Pre-cooked Hams and Sausages to reheat 165º F

Leftovers and Casseroles 165º F

Seafood (Fish and Shellfish) 145º F

Steak Doneness:

Rare (cool red center) 125º F
Medium Rare (warm red center) 135º F
Medium (warm pink center) 145º F
Medium Well (slightly pink center) 150º F
Well Done (little or no pink) 160º F

Egg Timer:

Soft Boiled: 5 minutes
Medium Boiled: 7 minutes
Hard Boiled: 9 minutes

Index of Recipes

T

V

Index of Photographs

A Jewish Home

Restaurants

My Thoughts on 65 Years of Cooking

Recipes

Typical (or not) Holiday Meals

Handy Hints

Cast of Characters

About the Author

Acknowledgments

Thanks to everyone mentioned in the stories, specifically included by name or not, who taught me cooking methods, secrets, or techniques that started me on my journey into cooking. Thanks to everyone who encouraged me, gave me suggestions of favorite meals, and recalled memories.

Thanks to my editor Dr. Alexandria Szeman, to Steve Bennett of Authorbytes, and to Charlie Levin, of Munn Avenue Press, for taking this old lady's hand and guiding me through this process. Special thanks to my daughter Rachel Thompson for her suggestions and guidance, as she knew I had something to say that was important for my children and grandchildren to know and remember, and it grew from there.

B'tay Ah Von!

Cast of Characters

Here's a short intro to our family tree.

Linda Carsman, wife of Gerald (Jerry) Carsman, mother of three daughters, grandmother (Bammy) of six, and great-grandmother of one.

Author Linda Carsman, age 3

Gerald (Jerry) Carsman, husband of Linda, father of three daughters, grandfather (Poppa) of six, and great-grandfather of one.

(Gerald) Jerry Carsman, age 3

The Daughters

Caren Carsman Sykes, eldest daughter.

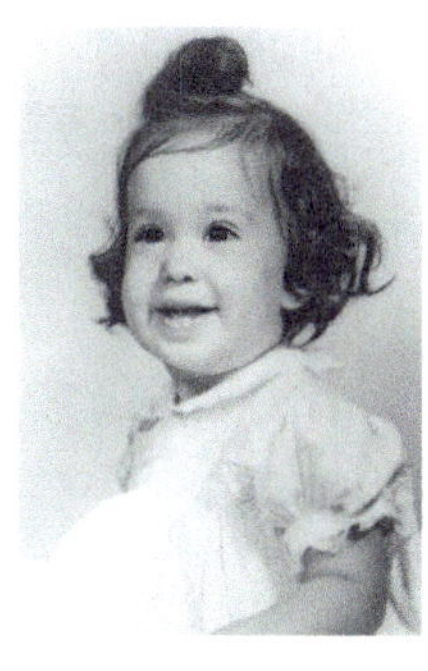

Caren Carsman Sykes, eldest daughter, age 1

Rachel Carsman Thompson, second daughter.

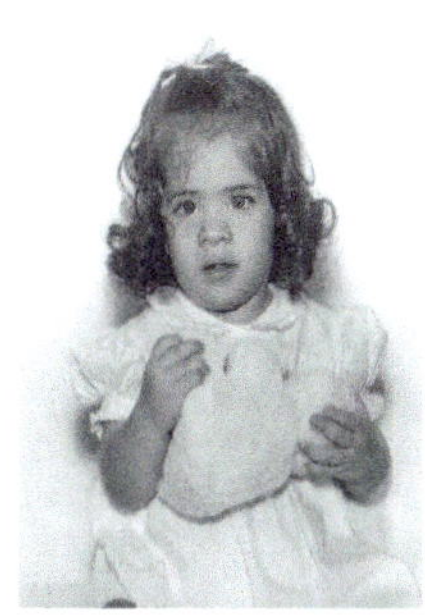

Rachel Carsman Thompson, second daughter, age 1

Leslie Carsman Hickey, youngest daughter.

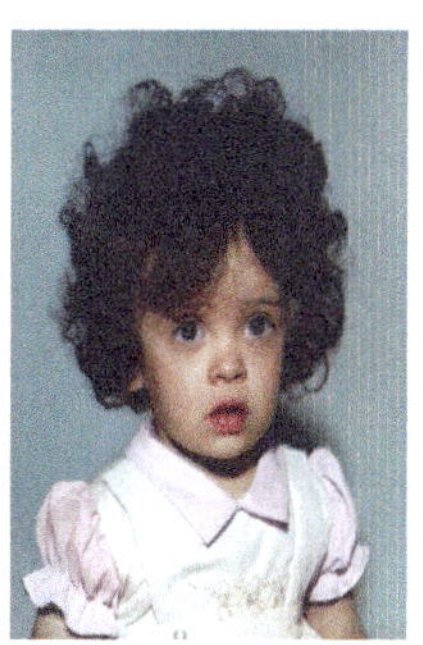

Leslie Carsman Hickey, youngest daughter, age 1

The Grandchildren

Sarah Sykes Walsh,
Caren's daughter.

Sarah Sykes Walsh,
Caren's daughter, age 3

Anya Thompson,
Rachel's daughter.

Anya Thompson,
Rachel's daughter, age 1

Lukas Thompson,
Rachel's son.

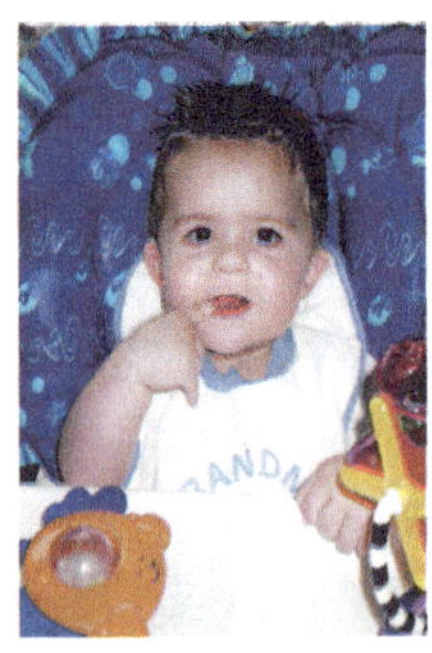

Lukas Thompson,
Rachel's son, age 1

Micah Hickey,
Leslie's eldest son.

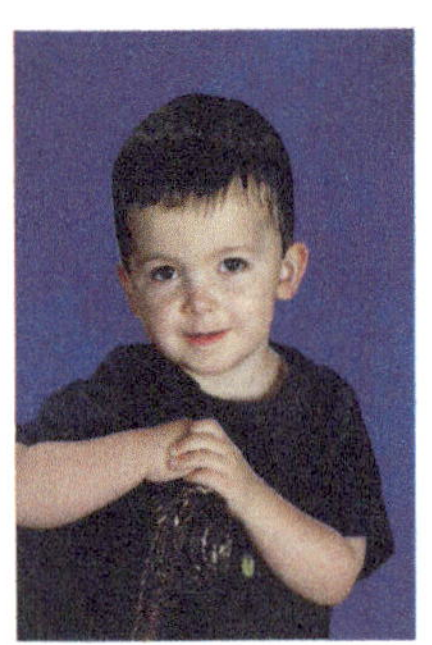

Micah Hickey,
Leslie's eldest son, age 3

Hannah Hickey,
Leslie's twin daughter.

Hannah Hickey,
Leslie's twin daughter, age 3

Elijah Hickey,
Leslie's twin son.

Elijah Hickey,
Leslie's twin son, age 3

The Great-Grandchild

Lael Walsh,
Sarah's daughter.

Lael Walsh,
Sarah's daughter, age 3

The Sons Who've Joined our Family

Chris Sykes, Caren's husband.
Jah Kaine, Rachel's partner.
Bryce Hickey, Leslie's husband.
Chris Walsh, Sarah's husband.

Linda's Immediate Family

Freda Harris, Linda's mother, "Bamma" to her grandchildren.
Leonard Harris, Linda's adopted father, "Poppy" to his grandchildren.
Jonathan Harris, Linda's brother.

Linda's Extended Family

Jacob Reich, Freda's father.
Clara Fritz Reich, Freda's mother.
Bertie Sherman, Rose Goldstein and **Lily Ann Blackoff**, Freda's sisters.
Abe Fritz, Freda's uncle and Clara's youngest brother.
Tillie Fritz, Uncle Abe's wife.
Anna Walt, Linda's aunt and oldest sister to Leonard Harris.

Jerry's Immediate Family

Morrie Carsman, Jerry's father.
Adele Frank Carsman, Jerry's mother.
Melvyn Carsman, Jerry's brother.

Jerry's Extended Family

Fern Fisher Frank, Adele's mother and Jerry's grandmother (Grandma).
Harry Frank, Adele's father and Jerry's grandfather (Zadie).
Ruth Trachtenberg, Jerry's aunt and sister to Morrie Carsman.
Ruth Carsman, Jerry's Aunt Ruthie, sister-in-law to Morrie Carsman and Ruth Trachtenberg, married to their youngest brother, David.

Other aunts, uncles, and cousins on both sides of the family, named in stories and others not named in this cooking memoir.

Friends

Marion Klein Bieksha, a dear friend of Linda and Jerry, wife of **Steve Klein,** Jerry's lifelong friend, Best Man, and husband of Marion.

About the Author

Linda Carsman,
Author photo by Kimberly S. Olker,
of Olker Photography

Linda Carsman loves her husband, her three daughters, her six grandchildren, and her one great-granddaughter, and the men who have become part of her family and enriched our lives beyond measure.

She considers herself a loving wife, mother, grandmother, family cook, avid reader, memory book creator, family photo collector, and now a writer.

Her idea of a vacation is planning the next meal while eating the current one with family and friends gathered nearby. Linda and Jerry traveled a bit after retirement and enjoyed their many cruises and vacations.

Linda, as a teenager, worked at her parent's Dairy Queen, where she was the Dilly Bar maker extraordinaire.

She was a Registered Radiologic Technologist, working both in Southern and Northern California, and then worked as a Parent Coordinator for the Elementary Intervention Program in the Psychological Services Department of a local school district. Her main job was meeting with the parents of the children in the program, teaching parenting skills, coordinating meals, and teaching parents the art and importance of family meals and experiences.

Website
InTheKitchenWithLindaCookbook

Facebook
LindaCarsmanMemoirCookbook

X (formerly Twitter)
KitchenWLinda

Instagram
LindaCarsmanMemoirCookbook

Made in the USA
Las Vegas, NV
05 October 2024